Lush Green Canopy
✦
Place of Refuge

poems and prose

Cyril A. Grant

Copyright © 2023 by Cyril A. Grant

All rights reserved solely by the author. The author guarantees all contents are original and do not infringe upon the legal rights of any other person or work.
No part of this publication may be reproduced, distributed, or transmitted in any form or by any means, including photocopying, recording, or other electronic or mechanical methods, without the prior written permission of the author.

ISBN: **979-8-218-95956-2**

First Edition: September 2023

Cover design and photography by Cyril A. Grant

Cotton Tree Press

Printed in the United States of America

NYAME DUA
"Tree of the Supreme Being"
A Tree of Presence and Protection

The tree as shade and symbol
As metaphor for life and family
As living history and beacon
Root, trunk, branch and leaf
Neglected...and ignored
Now scattered asunder

And our grief is bottomless
Our hope and certainty dashed
As we try to endure
Life, being and presence
All gone
To the place and paradise
Of our ancestors

Rest in our imaginations forever
Our beloved Cotton Tree

Contents

Introduction i

✦

Section One - Branches, Leaves and Fruits

Part 1 - Fritong 1

Freetown 2
Flotilla 4
Lush Green Canopy 6
Monuments and Relics 8
Rooted, Ruins and Resilience 12
The Cotton Tree City 15
Ekonomiks 21
The Orphanage, the Company and a Country - Fade to Black 22
Transformation 26
Ghosts 28
Futility 30
Crown Title 32
Broken, but Not Uprooted 34

Part 2 – Salon 39

All Is Not Lost 40
In Dependence Day 44
Wetin Du Wi Bah? 46
We 51
Welfare Bill 54
What We Need 56
Kush 59

Part 3 – Politricks 63

Oporto-nity 64
Peshawar - Baga - Garissa - Anywhere, Planet Earth 66
Tongues Tied 68
Power Trip 70

Wi Sɔri 72
Tweets and Vile Love Messages 73
Self-Evidents 75
Forgiveness 76
Settlers 78
Being Radical in Dreams Guarantees Everything? 80
Skin Deep 82
Window Fragment 84
My Brother's Keeper 86
Hands Off Our Tree Campaign 88
Lɛ I Pwɛl 90
Unrequited Love 92

✦

Section Two - Soil, Roots and Trunk
Part 1 - Fragility 97
Dust and Bone 98
Have You Ever? 100
Rest in Peace, Jamal 101
Are There Trees in Heaven? 102
Certainty   105
Return   107
Resting Place 108
Loss   110
Commander 113
Insomnia   114
Wi Yon Pɔrsin 114
Sharpness   118

Part 2 - Gratitude 121
Give Thanks 122
A New Year Starts Everyday 126
Dear Grandma 126
Dear Aunty Hawa 128
In Awe of the Night Sky 130
With Humility and Gratitude 126
Regional Power 134
Friendship   136

Instruction Manuals 138

Part 3 – Nostalgia 141

EJE 142
Inspired 146
Salon Bred 149
Vistas 153
Talking Trash 156
Addis Deities 160
Marriage Is No Mirage 162
For Those of Us with Black Suns 167
Lɛh Wi Pre 168

Notes 171

Endnotes 182

Images

Fritong
1 Maroon Church - Oldest in Freetown 3
2 Sunset - Tokeh Beach 5
3 The Regal Cotton Tree 7
4 Abandoned Edifice - Freetown, 2014 9
5 Freetown - Siaka Stevens Street Looking West 11
6 Fourah Bay College Original Building 12
7 Cityscape from the FCC Building 14
8 Krootown Road Market 16
9 Clock Tower 17
10 UpGun 20
11 Kekeh Traffic - Pademba Road 21
12 Governor's Gate - Wallace Johnson Street 23
13 Fade to Black 25
14 Steps from Wallace Johnson Street to Government Wharf 27
15 St. George's Cathedral 29
16 Wellington Street Edifice 31
17 Trinity Church, Kissy Road 33
18 Broken Tree 35
19 Sierra Leone Stamp 37
20 Powership at Sunset 38

Salon
21 After Run-Off Elections, 2018 41
22 Leather Rug - Late 20th Century, Mali 43
23 Sunset through Cotton Tree from State House, April 2021 45
24 Canoe at Fogbo Village 49
25 Sierra Leone Stamp 2 50
26 Makeni - Kabala Highway, 2021 51
27 Views to the Hills 53
28 Sunrise over Mount Auroel, 2021 55
29 Freetown, View from Tengbe Town 57
30 Tokeh Beach 60
31 Sunrise over the Cemetery Wall - Kingtom 61
32 Solitary Sunrise 62

Politricks
33 Sunset at Sussex Beach 65
34 Distant Sunrise 67
35 Sovereign Tongues 68
36 CLSG Power Substation - Kenema 71
37 Tweet Bird on Red with Star Bullet Holes 73
38 Bod Ose - Pademba Road and Bathurst Street 77
39 George Street House 79
40 King Jimmy Harbour 81
41 Red Grass Flower - Port Loko 83
42 Bullet Hole through Window 85
43 Royal Post Box - Hennessey Street, Kingtom 86
44 Cotton Tree Stump, Cloudy Day 89
45 Pultney Street - Towards Kroo Bay 91
46 Water Pressure – Patton Street 93
47 Sierra Leone Stamp 3 94

Fragility
48 Dad. Ascension Cemetery 99
49 Sun Flower Sketch 102
50 Wild Flower – Moyamba, September 2022 104
51 Buried Cannon - Wallace Johnson/Gloucester Streets 106
52 Circular Road Cemetery 109
53 Wild Flowers - Ridgewood, NJ 111
54 Plaque - Governor's Gate - Wallace Johnson Street 112
55 House on Charles Street 115
56 Bai Bureh Ferry at Government Wharf 117
57 Mother's Memorial Wreath 119
58 Ston Ose - Opposite Krootown Road Market 120

Gratitude
59 Baby C, 3 or 4 Months Old, 1962 123
60 Hibiscus - Aqua Club, 2022 125
61 Ethel Matilda Ashwood - nee, Malamah-Thomas* 127
62 Traditional Gazebo - Tiama 129
63 Full Moon. Freetown, 2020 131
64 Sussex Beach, 2021 133

65 Africa - Colonial Dessert*** 135
66 Night Lights over Freetown, 2022 137
67 Yellow Bell - Maroon Church Yard 139
68 Cathedral House 140

Nostalgia
69 Eustace Josephus Ekundayo Ashwood, 1898 - 1974* 143
70 Red Lion through Window - Kingtom 145
71 Ashwood Family, 1952* 146
72 Adah Grant, nee Johnson* 147
73 Gracie, Pamela, Jestina and Gloria - 1980's* 148
74 Red Lion House, 1948 – 13 Bolling Street, Kingtom* 150
75 Salon Bred 151
76 Malamah House 152
77 Malamah House Interiors 156
78 Malamah House Staircase 157
79 Washed Ashore - Lumley Beach 159
80 Injera - Addis Ababa, March 2023 161
81 November 4th 1961* 163
82 Variegated Hibiscus, 2012 165
83 The Suns - Football Stars 166
84 Railway Bridge behind Gibraltar Church 169

All images taken or created by the Author
Except for these marked
*Family Archives
**From https://vafrica.africa/old-fourah-bay-college/
*** From https://commons.wikimedia.org/wiki/
File:Flag_map_of_Colonial_Africa_(1913).png

Introduction

Lush Green Canopy refers to the striking, majestic Cotton Tree at the centre of Freetown, Sierra Leone, on the west coast of Africa. The Tree, a national monument, has borne witness to the country's most pivotal moments, and survived natural disasters, fires, and human activity for over 230 years.

The **Place of Refuge,** Freetown, was created in 1787 as Granville Town under the patronage of British abolitionists of the Slave Trade, with the settlement of 400 freed "Blacks" and destitute individuals from London. The town was burned down in 1790, and rebuilt and resettled by the Sierra Leone Company in 1792, with 1,100 Nova Scotians. The Nova Scotians, formerly enslaved military conscripts, had been granted freedom and land as compensation for fighting with British Loyalists in the American Revolution. Unhappy with the circumstances of life in Northern Canada and disappointed with the pledged land grants, they lobbied and secured support for the cross-Atlantic journey back to the "Province of Freedom", Sierra Leone.

A 15-ship flotilla left the Canadian Atlantic coastline in January 1792 and arrived three months later in March. The new settlers cleared the land and celebrated their providence with a service of thanksgiving under a cotton tree near the harbour, and the area was christened "Free Town". In 1800, the town was significantly enlarged by the arrival of 500 Maroons from Jamaica, shipped into exile by the British Crown.

Between 1808 and 1863, Freetown, the then capital of British West Africa, served as the base for the British Royal Navy's West Africa Squadron; tasked with enforcing the prohibition of the slave trade.

The Squadron intercepted itinerant ships and their human cargo; through these efforts, thousands of recaptured and liberated Africans found sanctuary and built new lives in Sierra Leone. The liberated Africans and returning settlers, who were ethnically and religiously diverse, evolved into the "Creole People" with a distinct Krio Language, which has now become the "lingua franca" of Sierra Leone. The Creoles of Freetown are also known as the Krios.

Freetown, Sierra Leone, and the Cotton Tree loom large in this collection of poems. The themes I write about include family, legacy, loss, gratitude, friendship, politics, and Krio identity; all of which can be seen through the metaphors of "Cotton Tree Canopy" and "Place of Refuge".

No one could have predicted the Tree's demise during a torrential rainstorm on the 25th of May 2023, and the subsequent psychological effect on Freetown and its inhabitants. Some regard it as a bad omen for the peace and tranquillity of the city and country. Others see it finally sealing the fate and demise of the Krio people and their influence. I, however, find it fortuitous to be alive at this moment, bearing witness to the hopes and aspirations of our ancestors who for generations relied on the certainty of the Tree and their lasting presence in Freetown. This physical and emotional devastation is a reminder of the impermanence and unpredictability of life and gives pause for reflection.

The Cotton Tree has always been an inspiring presence and part of my cultural DNA. As a little boy, I walked past it every day after school, on my way to my grandfather's office, within the reaches of the Tree's shadow. Coincidentally as I write this now, several decades later, my office, located at the end of a corridor on the 5th Floor of Electricity House faces the historic site. Two photographs within this book; one before the disaster, and the other after, were taken from this vantage point.

Freetown has retained its ethnic, cultural and religious diversity and its Tree has emerged as a symbol of direction, identity, shade and refuge, both for the minority Krio, and the country at large. It is an appropriate metaphor, as family and country provide canopy and shade beneath which individuals endure the fragility of life, loss, and the celebration of milestones and transitions.

A tree expands as new generations are born with each branch representing a different lineage, yet all are connected to the same trunk. These generations, evolving through phases and seasons of adversity and prosperity, adapt and thrive, leaving behind a legacy of values and memories that endure. Similarly, just as a tree draws strength and sustenance from its roots, a family's roots lie in its ancestors, traditions and shared history; a foundation for growth and development.

The Cotton Tree and its ensuing history also inspired the organization of this book into two sections. **Section 1 – Branches, Leaves and Fruits** are the outward themes in three parts: **Fritong, Salon** and **Politricks**. **Section 2 – Soil, Roots and Trunk** are the inner, more intimate and personal themes, also in 3 parts: **Fragility, Gratitude** and **Nostalgia**.

I hope that these writings speak to the interconnectedness, continuity, and strength that can be found within a supportive and nurturing family, loyal friendships and among upstanding citizens. I am also drawn to the dysfunction and pain within these social bonds, which provide an equivalent wellspring of creative expression.

Without a doubt, I am proud of the contributions, sacrifices and example of my Ancestors and our unique stories...out of the horror of history, we still rise. Their legacies, without apology or deference, continue to inspire. Freetown, Sierra Leone and the World will continue to evolve, but change for the better is what we all seek; change that creates space for progress, prosperity, inclusion and appreciation of differences in culture and points of view.

Acknowledgements

Sincere gratitude to my wife, Olivia, and our two sons, Kobina and Kwame. They are my constant shade and centre, keeping me rooted and loved. Olivia has always encouraged my poetry and prose. She is my original muse and still treasures the very first poem I wrote to her, when we met over 30 years ago. She has always believed in my abilities, and of course, still corrects my gaffes when necessary.

My parents are prominent inspirations for me also. I lost my Father when I was just three years old, and I trust he would be proud of this collection. My Mother, a raconteur extraordinaire, with a larger-than-life personality, passed away a decade ago. Mom had the gift of expression and storytelling, and an intrinsic ability to find humour and life lessons in even the most mundane of experiences.

My siblings, Bryan and Desiree, give me strength and unbridled support always. They have been good sounding boards for ideas and direction.

Sylvester and Juliana Rowe, my adopted in-laws and surrogate parents all-in-one, have been an inspiration and a moral compass for over 30 years. They are ardent admirers of my writing and provided invaluable assistance with the Krio translations and commentary.

Tani and Daphne Pratt have been the fire and challenge; pushing me this far, eliciting a promise on my part to publish.

I dedicate this book to Kobina and Kwame; they are the fulfilment of my hopes and ambition: independent, kind, grounded and loving young men. I have faith in their generation: post 9-11, post-Ebola, post-COVID, experiencing Trump, Boris, the Russia-Ukraine Conflict, the explosion of AI capability and use…the list goes on. May they continue to believe in themselves and in their innate abilities to thrive and to succeed, as inheritors of resilience, courage and the poetry of life.

Finally, and always, I feel a deep appreciation for our Ancestors known and unknown…for the miracles and coincidences that created the lives we all live, and for the providence and blessings that come my way constantly.

Rest in Power and in Peace….
Cyril A. Grant
Freetown
September 2023

✦

There is a vast bibliography on Freetown and the Creoles/Krios. These days, the internet brings knowledge to your fingertips and several Wikipedia URL's provide adequate summaries and counterpoints:

1. https://futuretreehealth.com.au/cotton-tree-sierra-leone (July, 2023)
2. https://en.wikipedia.org/wiki/Sierra_Leone_Company (2023)
3. https://en.wikipedia.org/wiki/Freetown (2023)
4. https://en.wikipedia.org/wiki/Timeline_of_Freetown#Bibliography (2023)

For deeper scholarship and understanding, there are a range of books, but the primary sources are the following:

1. Akintola Wyse: *The Krio of Sierra Leone: An Interpretive History*. London: Hurst in association with the International African Institute, 1989
2. Arthur T. Porter: *Creoledom: A Study of the Development of Freetown Society*, Oxford University Press, 1963
3. Christopher Fyfe: *A History of Sierra Leone*. London: Oxford University Press, 1962

Section One

Branches, Leaves and Fruits

Part 1 - Fritong

Freetown

More than any other place in the world, this is where the effects of the 400-year-old trade came to rest

Where men and women of conscience sought to repent from the sins of brutality on Africans

Where Africans, off slave ships on the high seas, were liberated

Where settlers from Nova Scotia who dreamed of a return

Where the "troublesome" Maroons from Jamaica were shipped

Where the black and poor in London were given a new lease on life

Freetown

A blossoming flower that has been sacked and burnt
Over and over again

Freetown, where the Koya still dispute the land purchase and governments continue to squeeze its scrotum, questioning its legitimacy, demanding subservience to politics and party

Where the descendants of those Liberated Africans survive…
And where their rights and being continue to be questioned and denied

Where politics has inhaled and continuously, systematically expunges every trace and achievement of those proud liberated commodities.

Freetown
A place we still call home.

Fritong

1 Maroon Church - Oldest in Freetown

Flotilla

Thunder roared all round in the depthless darkness
As lightning hammers flashed and zig-zagged across the sky
The wind billowed in anger against the crashing waves, lifting the puny vessels up, defying gravity
Then smashed them with abandon, violently through the uncertain watery surface.

They had been at sea for two months;
And Halifax a distant memory.
Sailing east towards the sun with hope
Towards the prodigal continent and refuge.

These were no ordinary seafarers, but battled hardened Loyalists of Empire
Looking forward to justice denied and liberty at last
In the Province of Freedom.

They dreamed of the land and the sky
Of finally tasting free
Away from the desolate, cold winters of the North Atlantic shores

The flotilla inched its way along the waters;
Resting place at its depths for the thousands of commodities fortuitously claimed, in transit
Depriving traders of added bounty and treasure of black gold.
Fifteen ships in total, outfitted and stocked for the pilgrimage and settlement.

Fritong

Over a thousand hopeful souls, searching the horizon each day for the rays of the dawn.
Each with a silent prayer of faith for blessings and salvation

2 Sunset - Tokeh Beach

For landing at their
Jerusalem at last

Hearts bursting
Joyful at a chance
For a new beginning.

Lush Green Canopy

Lush green canopy
Majestic, with regal trunk and branches
Framed by blue skies…and white bucolic clouds
Sits centre over the city
The connections of this framed vista are so many.

In the foreground a train station, turned national museum,
sits…unambitious and lacking
But a repository nonetheless of the many peoples Serra Lyoa[1]

In the background, sneaking through…the edifice of the Law…
Former seat of the Admiralty granting freedoms after benefitting from 300 years of the trade
Conscience, philanthropy or usefulness expired?

A beautiful Monday morning, nonetheless, as the city awakens…
Each citizen hawker oblivious to the surrounding grandeur and history.

There are no wisps of tear gas now
No tears-or-wrists in defiance
Just rays of sunshine showering down the honks of kekes[2]
Everyone on their journey, anticipating the next thunderstorm
And the rainbow that surely will form.

Blessings and Peace be ever thine own
Land that we Love.

Fritong

3 The Regal Cotton Tree

Monuments and Relics

With its rundown wooden houses
Narrow streets...samba gutters[3]
Sagging, sparking confetti of old telephone and electric lines
Rusty tin shack communities hugging the bays and shorelines
Creeping in all directions, up the surrounding hills and valleys
With splendorous views of the Atlantic
And the infinite horizon

In all those liberated villages, now transformed...now coalesced into an endless sprawl.
Lies Freetown.

Faded beauty
Neglected soul.

She surprises still in quiet moments
Descending from Krootown Road to Kingtom Bridge
Or the sudden vista at Upgun on leaving Kissy Road
Sometimes, the curved entry to Congo Cross
The race down Hillcot Road
Even Bɔmɛh[4], a behemoth now, exudes a certain melancholy
You will catch your breath, and suddenly realise, that yet still, through all this, is a beating, passionate heart

Cradle of Freedom
Crucible of Creoledom
Womb of the formerly captive

4. Abandoned Edifice -Freetown, 2014

Congo, Aku, Loko, Maroon, Yoruba, Ashanti, Igbo, Mende, Limba,
Fulani, Vai, Sherbro, Soso, Temne, Kissi, Kono, Kuranko,
Krim, Bullum, Mandingo, Kosso
This melting pot, simmers with parishes and their churches; mosques and their unambitious minarets, side by side
A city though, with limited tolerance.

Formerly meritorious, now reduced to rubble…with WhatsApp speeches and philosophy
Mt. Auroel looms large from every angle, a testament to the vision, and achievements of a lettered past.

Together with the Cotton Tree, this city of monuments and relics is slowly disappearing…replaced by garish, confident tiled structures, with wide-brimmed, expensive and soulless edifices
There are no neighbours here on Fourah Bay Road, Wellington Street, Naimbana or Priscilla streets

Free Town is sinking…it cannot escape the weight of concrete, shit-strewn gutters, where rivers of plastic spill over, making their way to the mouth of the river, kissing the sea.

Pa Demba and King Tom of the Koya are long gone
So too are those proud generations…striving to create a culture
A new life…where the law negotiated and guaranteed
One's boundary and being.

Our roots run deep, but the streams have evaporated, exposing the red laterite and rock.

We need rain, plenty rain and many more planting seasons to recover.

Fritong

5 Freetown - Siaka Stevens Street Looking West

Rooted, Ruins and Resilience

In the foreground
Waters of the Freetown harbour, and slightly up above the shoreline,
a desolate, solid brick edifice in ruin.

Out of place in this modern vista, is the venerated
Fourah Bay College, our faded beauty and heritage.

6 Fourah Bay College Original Building

And everywhere, filling the hills of the background…sprouting without plan or foresight, are the new fragile, but permanent growths…home and abode to the many, eking out fortunes and daily ten tawzin[5] green notes.

Migrants from lands and villages afar, propelled by the War, or the
pull and promise of a better life, have secured land or rent that room
en pala[6]

Similarly, our ancestors came, but bundled and tied in ships
Hopeless and lost, yet some with mission and yearning
To this haven, cradle of freedom
With African sensibility and tone
To thrive and blossom…planting roots, growing branches, sprouting
flowers and fruit of a vibrant culture.

The waters of the Rokel lap endlessly on the Freedom shore, as it
meets and mates with the great Atlantic, reminding us
Each wave a tick of time…silent sentinels
The hills in the distance cradle this city that has aged immodestly
With fragile veins, its heart pumping slowly
We are reminded that there are dreams here still, in spite of all the
jagged edges of existence and loathing.

Let us therefore take pause and give thanks
For sacrifices and love
For tears and fears that created a land of promise
Steeped in Law, rooted in culture and learning
A resilient people with a never-ending, brimming confidence to
believe in themselves and the future.

Blessings upon you, dearly departed
Freetown lives still, but differently
With thanks and praise, everlasting.

7 Cityscape from the FCC Building

The Cotton Tree City

We hardly produce anything now as a nation...and that is quite apparent in the capital, Freetown – a microcosm and melting pot of this land and people...all too human, with dreams and aspirations for improvement in this life, or in the next.

And the main activities for business or trading rely on what is discarded, used by the West...the remnant value, high in this economy.

There is a certain sadness, a resignation really...a city reduced to second hand status of clothes on our backs, shoes on our feet...and cheap colourful Chinese knockoffs.

But a vibrancy also, all too familiar in a modern African city
Despite the lack of a social net, little industry...or productive activity, there exists a constant recycling of products and lives and faded, torn currency...day in and out.
Everywhere you look in this city of dreams, there are people going on with their daily existences, eking out a living, making a go of it. A walk or drive in the city centre, west to east, is a pastiche of experiences...all your senses are engaged.

The provision shops on Krootown Road are full of evaporated or powdered milk tins, sardines, sachets of coffee or milk strung up, yellow bata[7] of vegetable oil, sugar cubes, toilet paper, corn flakes, frozen chicken from Brazil, vacuum flasks, bags and bags of imported rice and onions.

By the market further down, the women and girls sit gossiping, confident, each with an extension or wig, or cornrows neat and natural...surrounded by heaps of pepper, onions, barrels of gari, beans, rice, chicken parts, cowfut, pigfut, meat, baskets of coal, Maggi cubes, bundles of plasas[8], tin tamatis[9].

8 Krootown Road Market

Or closer to Choitrams Supermarket, traders with luscious vegetables and fruits: cucumbers, melon, mangoes, carrots, Irish potatoes and salad stalks...or up Edwards Street by Sanders Street; open stalls of building materials, paints, tins of paint, sand paper, screw drivers, padlocks, nails, zinc sheets, recycled electrical cable.

A little further on Siaka Stevens Street, after Jokey Bridge, past the shiny new Ecobank, more formal...electrical stores, staffed by Indian men on two-year contracts...filled with wire and lightbulbs, fans, freezers, generators, gas stoves, LED smart TVs of every size, irons, and ironing boards.

Or on Pademba Road, after 5 p.m., filled with street hawkers, young men and women – preteens really, selling brushes, brooms, steering wheel covers and mats, led torch lights, sunglasses, patriotic Sierra Leone flag pins, or groundnut parched or boiled, peeled oranges, packets of plantain chips, and machine bread, six packets to a hand, waving at the traffic, dashing in between printing shops and a smattering of pharmacies...we see the old Bod Os dɛm[10], sentries of grandeur past, sitting silently, rotting away.

Then down to the famous "Belgium" Area, by Connaught Hospital, where throngs of hustling young men sell phones, TVs, game consoles, furniture, bicycles, tricycles, toddler battery cars, prams, football boots – strung by their laces, suitcases of every stripe and colour...or by Charlotte Street, by Swissy, the old jewellery shop, are men also, with sling bags, constantly waving down the prosperous or JC looking passer-by for forex.

Up Gloucester Street, by the post office, a specialty stalls of maps, books and pens and all kinds of writing pads and stationary...ending up at lower Siaka Stevens Street, full of electronic and phone stores...you then encounter the complexity of the PZ area, the shoe bazaar and buses, transport to all destinations east...ending eventually at Ecowas Street; full of building materials shops that sandwich the junks sellers; mostly used clothes, fresh from the barrels, crowding out the street, choked up...or down Sani Abacha Street, where traffic is reduced to a crawl, and vendors of all merchandise fill the pavement, in a life-and-death competition with the shops

Or down Regent Road where the Nigerian men, former ECOMOG[11] boys, have shops for spare parts…tires, horns, alternators, batteries, headlights; all genuine, they claim.

And at Clock Tower, the mass of vendors, overwhelming, congregating, flowing to Kissy Road or Fourah Bay Road…lively people all about with poda-poda[12] and kɛkɛs[13] locked in battle for movement and fares.

And every shop to Up-Gun, overflowing with the detritus of Abroad…used mattresses, carpets, toys, cutlery, picture frames, furniture, TVs, stereos, computers, cabinets – virtually a container and barrel superstore…count the number of children selling water, or food…carrying trays and boxes on their heads…walking in competition with each other for the one or two thousand Leones…hardly enough profit for the day.

The ebb and tide of people along the main arteries are nonstop…all have a story, all have a destination, all have dreams in this Cotton Tree City, this free town.

This is home to us all…dusty, tired worn out…our city will survive, our city will revive itself, clean itself and slowly, our Cotton Tree City, with its deep roots and branches, will bloom.

No longer a junk-strewn place, but a productive city, heralding the transformation of its people and land beyond, to every part of Lion Mountain Country, itself.

Fritong

9 Clock Tower

10 UpGun

Fritong

Ekonomiks

Krootown Road
Tuesday morning traffic at 9:30 a.m. towards Kingtom Bridge:

45 kekes[14] and 6 taxis
No podapoda
That's a total of 51 jobs carrying 108 passengers
Equivalent to 3 buses: 6 jobs or
6 podapodas[15]: 12 jobs

11 Kekeh Traffic – Pademba Road

45 kekes[16] mean 90 liters of petrol
Increased traffic jams and inhaled exhaust fumes

Like the invisible plastic bottles and bags that litter our gutters.
Particles of smoke in our lungs and, low-skill driving jobs must mean progress, no?

But, at what cost?

The Orphanage, the Company and a Country Fade to Black

You are an orphan…
Actually, stolen from your parents, from your village and sold off far away
You somehow manage to survive, with little education, but tons of grit, determination and faith
Working for years at a Company, for very little pay

Everyone knows your story
At some point, the Company decides to make amends
They find some land near where you were born
Buy it, and give you Title
In fact, they prohibit the sale of orphans on the high seas and give them all collective ownership to this land.

You establish a town and despite the hardships, you create a culture and an oasis for you and your descendants.

You thrive.

A few years later, the surrounding villages and towns clamour to have their statuses elevated from being Protected to full Colony.

The Company decides that it would be better if you blend your town with the surrounding villages to be granted a new status.
You protest and complain that your newly gained rights would evaporate in this amalgamation.

The Company would not hear of it, saying: it is for your own good.

Fritong

12 Governor's Gate – Wallace Johnson Street

You agree, hoping a new nation would emerge, a new destiny for all its people:
Unity, Freedom and Justice.

Over the years the new amalgamation also thrives,
With this free town now the sovereign capital
However, as luck would have it
You slowly lose influence and prestige
Your children move away.

Somehow, all the institutions and values you created, built up over 200 years evaporate.

In fact, your principles, approach to life and learning are derided
Your culture and manner despised
You can no longer aspire to political office, without virulent attack and bullying.

It takes a while, but you come to a realization,
Settlers have never been welcomed
Just tolerated.

It was just a matter of time,
But there are no new directions for us.

Virtual genocide is real
No nation, no people, no destiny, no country
Just pure sacking of any trace of you and your origins
Fade to black.
No tears
No anger
Just pure irrelevance

The End.

Fritong

13 Fade to Black

Transformation

My aunt returned after 20 something years away
To a different count-ree now!

A very African city like Lagos or Kinshasa…sprawling and
spiralling out of control

Now tattered and worn at the seams
No longer the Krio town it used to be
That Caribbean enclave on the rice coast
Complete with resettled Maroons, Nova Scotians
And high seas
Re-captives from factories and forts, dotting the coast;
Elmina, Cape Coast, Goree, Nassau, Cormantin,
St. Louis, James Fort, Secondi and Dix Cove

With wide, orderly streets given names like
Trelawny, Westmoreland, Pultney, Percival, Liverpool,
Walpole, Charlotte, Howe, Gloucester, Wellington,
Waterloo, Bathurst

Streets weaving and connecting East and West
Sojah Tong, Kroo Tong, Maroon Tong, Portuguese Tong,
Congo and Kosso Tongs

Each distinct settlement sprinkled between the main wharf and
the bays:
Susan's Bay, Destruction Bay, Foura Bay
With bridges over valleys framing streams and waterfalls
Flowing right through from those Lion Mountain peaks.

That colony, that freedom chalice
Has transformed in time and tone.
It's a different count-ree now!

Fritong

14 Steps from Wallace Johnson Street to Government Wharf

Ghosts

Many, many years from today
After every inch of its hills are colonised again, but this time in the name of local content, and appeasement of landless citizens whose governments and politrickcians have failed and betrayed them

We will find among the smoking ruins, remnants of a people disappeared.
Their ghosts will still roam the streets, valleys and bays…
Unable to claim abode or rest
In this town secured for enduring life and liberty.

Proud, resilient souls they were…flawed in many ways
But oh, did they engrain the shores of this peninsula with vision and promise.

Derided for being
For existing
For thriving
For spinning gold out of grief and abandonment.
We will evaporate from this place, from this free town.

Our graves will sink with the weight of history
But the memories and willpower, integrity of heart and purpose
The never-ending belief in learning, self-improvement and self-assurance…will linger
In testament everlasting over this fading relic

A decaying monument to earth's history of bondage and Freedom.

Fritong

15 St. George's Cathedral

Futility

Making the case for Freetown, no less the Western Area
After 60 plus years of in-dependence is a journey in futility

With the sprawl of wealth and concrete
Ghastly cuts of roadways up hills
Uprooted trees in every valley
Empty palaces blooming in every direction
Slowly choking the vistas and beauty of a land in claim by everyone
Unprotected crown or, dare I say, settler heritage.

The land has become proxy for the never-ending colour battle
Red and green
Protecting their heritage, but giving free range and title to all asunder.

Raw sewage and plastic float down valleys
And every corner boasts an outdoor market with mega phones blasting…selling junks and provisions and cookery with dubious oils and meat.

From sea to beach to valley and hill, as far as the eye can see,
joblo jabla[17]

Development has become death

But, we move.

Fritong

16 Wellington Street Edifice

Crown Title

All this time
The protectorate has been fuming
Over the freedom of the crown colony lands
And the imperious attitude of the rotten cassava eaters.

How those white imposters
Were given title and free reign
Over Sabanoh[18].
Deep-seated resentment
Over the airs of former chattel
Lording it for centuries over the nobles
Hailing from rich, interior heritages.

Now we see how this inadequacy has festered
Rejecting whyte, Yoruba or Akan-named settlers
Who with starched shirts and printed camisoles
Dared to strut their words and knowledge and book
After all, the purchase was coerced from illiterate Koya royalty

So these claims of crown lands and protected heights are now
Invalidated in red and green ink.
How do you appease the hungry and desperate masses?
Make them feel special…equal and above those African imposters?

Infringement on rights, a tried and tested solution
Free title sprinkled on every corner
Dismantle the crown, remove the jewels, grind the gold to dust
Erase all history of belonging of a people Resettled.

We move blindly into the future
All peoples, no country
No direction.

Fritong

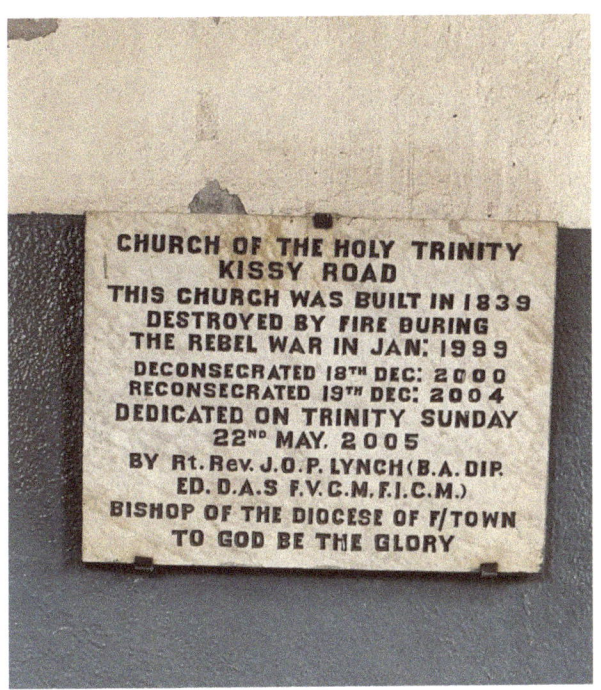

17 Trinity Church, Kissy Road

Broken, But Not Uprooted

The itch to cash in on the "Salon" heritage, to replace the broken Cotton Tree with an appropriate monument, is increasing in volume with all sorts of proposals sprouting in our imaginations; probably decked in brightly coloured swag…garishly lit with solar LEDs, programmed to switch colours; green, white and blue incessantly, to remind those of us with defective short-term memory, of our national flag.

But there is no more poignant and powerful a national monument than the remaining stump…in all its jagged and brutal beauty, to remind us of the impermanence and unpredictability of life.

Strangely also, it is the perfect monument to all those departed souls; landed, freed, granted solace…who created a thriving culture and presence in the Freetown peninsula, despite the odds.

The Tree is a Freetown Settler as well.

Imagine the feelings of the Nova Scotians…having fought with life and limb for the British in the American Revolution, promised – then denied – solace, languishing in that difficult clime until granted a new beginning here

Or the many fierce Maroons; troublemaker warriors, shipped to quell their dangerous tendencies against the Crown and plantation owners in Jamaica

Fritong

18 Broken Tree

Or the many black and white indigents from London, given a second birth and chance on this peninsula

Or the thousands of African men, women and children…sold to slaving ships up and down the coast, from Senegal to Angola, from factories and slave forts that dot the coastlines…recaptured by the Admiralty, processed and set free, steps from the root of the tree.

Even Sengbe Pieh, a hero, must have been emotional on return to these shores, on seeing this marker of freedom and home.

There is no Freetown without the Cotton Tree and indeed, no Sierra Leone without Freetown.

The Tree looms large in Krio identity, and of Sierra Leone as a nation.
It is central to our idea of citizenship, the focus and physical unifier of government; radiating out to the Executive, Legislative, Judiciary and Citizenry, equally providing the virtual pivot of our history and the possibilities of our future.

Broken, but still rooted, this event and change gives us time as citizens to reconsider the natural monument's veneration and proper place in our imagination of nationhood and in acknowledgement of the significance of our history.

No longer should it be a backdrop for government posters or party announcements. The tree sits in what we can all acknowledge is a Krio Heritage Circle, as well as the epicentre of Sierra Leone.

Fritong

This should be our Independence Square, our Lincoln Memorial.

Indeed, Freetown and Sierra Leone have transformed over the 230 years since the city's foundation. The Krios are no longer the dominant group in this town, or in national politics. However, there is no question of their past and continued presence and contributions to this country and the idea of Sierra Leone nationhood. We are indeed a single nation of many origins and cultures.

19 Sierra Leone Stamp

At this time in history, we are a fragile and fractured nation
Broken, but not uprooted
It is time to nurture our stump, rekindle our memories, acknowledge and appreciate our histories and contributions.

May Blessings and Peace be ever our own.
May our Ancestors be exalted in this
Land that we Love.

20 Powership at Sunset

Part 2 – Salon

All Is Not Lost

All is not lost, because
Throughout the length and breadth of this land
There are citizens committed to their work and vocation
Who get up each morning with integrity and purpose
Without regard for party or tribe or family connection
Without regard for accolade or social status.
These men and women believe in tomorrow
They believe in Unity, Freedom and Justice.

They are teachers, messengers, drivers, farmers, police and army
nobodies, market women, street hawkers, civil servants of all stripes,
Omolankay[19] pushers, bankers, doctors, lawyers…engineers
Incredibly talented citizens
All sorts of people who work ceaselessly
Without envelopes or bribes
Without facilitation fees
Without compromise.

These are the real heroes of our democracy
They are not wealthy by any means
But their consciences and hearts are clean.

All is not lost
For we believe these citizens
Small in number, will become the new standard for our country.
If we are indeed to move forward
To restore civility and merit
We must all endeavour to become like these role models
Putting Sierra Leone first before tribe or party.

Salon

The new leadership should be visionary enough to galvanize citizens, all.

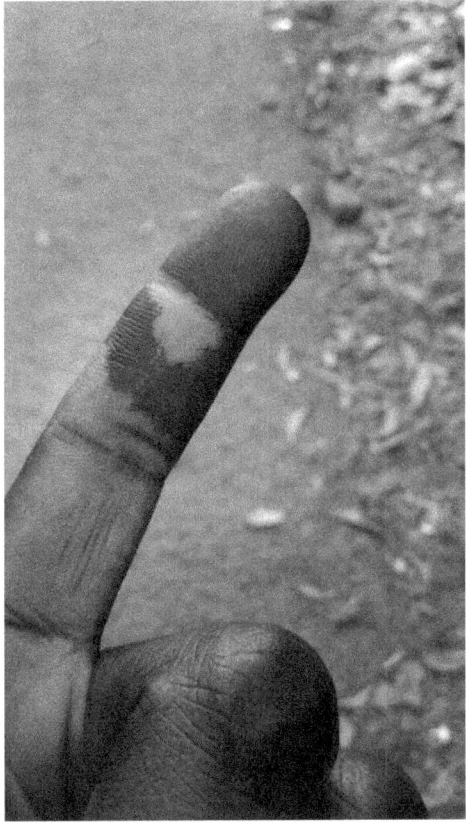

21 After Run-off Elections, 2018

The work and sacrifice of our living heroes, playing by the rules with hope for a better tomorrow, should inspire us to do better.
To be better
To become better citizens every day.

We Sierra Leoneans deserve healthcare,
Not death sentences...

We Sierra Leoneans deserve schools and education,
Not factories of functional illiterates.

We Sierra Leoneans deserve universities that produce the best and brightest, with graduates that are creative, not afraid of manual work and are critical thinkers.

Enough of the grovelling, and shuffling and scheming for handouts...enough of the patronage of knowledge and wealth. Enough of the fake degrees, bought certificates and half-baked thinking.

Enough of the ill-conceived projects...
And siphoning of donor funding
To line our pockets and the hills of Freetown.

The future is in our heads
But we fear our potential,
And even more,
The potential of every other Sierra Leonean.

That, is the true tragedy...
Being afraid of what we can truly become.

With hard work and courage,
We Sierra Leoneans
Will create with our hands and minds
A society that harbours
Opportunity for all.

Salon

There is nothing magical about this.

All is not lost
For everywhere
There is a spark, a person
Who believes
And works tirelessly

22 Leather Rug - Late 20th Century, Mali

For a new reality.
Our better days are yet to come.
Indeed, all is not lost.

In Dependence Day

Standing on the grounds of the former Fort Thornton.
The flags have been lowered.
The National Anthem is playing...we are solemn, erect...giving honour to country.

Over the ramparts to the west, is the setting sun, beyond the Cotton Tree.

This 60th year has seen our spirits dampened
Corona, loss of friends and family...uncertainty...an anaemic economy...a discouraged diaspora
Threats and counter-threats by bikers and official guards.

In the fading notes of the anthem
"Blessing and Peace be ever thine own"
One is overcome by emotion, thinking of
Ancestors, all...those original inhabitants of the coast and the interior... joined by migrants from north and east, by land and sea.
From Mali, Futa Jallon, forests of the east, Songhai
Those who were brought here and liberated
Those who sailed from Nova Scotia or London, on the promise of freedom
We are an amalgamation
Years in nation-craft, much in the making...but, as we are acutely aware, there's still much to be done

The setting sun, glowing...outlines our navel tree
Looking forward to a new day
We owe our Ancestors eternal optimism

Happy In Dependence Day
In Advance.

Salon

23 Sunset through Cotton Tree from State House, April 2021

Wetin Du Wi Bah?[20]

Where to begin
To engage, to rant about our peculiar problems as a nation
To again scream out loud about our lack
Lack of patriotism
Lack of imagination
Lack of will to do right
Lack of national or personal integrity
Lack of leadership…in all areas: religion, education, the law…governance
Lack of love.

Of course, these may exist in various spaces, bɔt bra, wi nɔr de fil am oh[21]!
It is, at once, a surreal and painful experience to visit other countries on the continent that are pushing forward
Getting it right
Making a nation out of its many
Its citizens showing pride and dignity in carriage and speech…and all this manifest before us in infrastructure, institutions, education…development
Not perfect by any means; but you go kɔle[22]!!

This is not an anti-party rant
This is a rant about the Elephant in the Room in all our conversations, about the lack of all things Sierra Leone and in Sierra Leoneans
Each one of us has the obligation to be angry at the state of our nationhood.
Angry at the pendulum politics of revenge, of exclusion, the politics of pokitricks, the politics of "wan place dancing"[23]
Angry at all "dɛn sai wɛ dɛn tai cow, dan de dɔn bɔhku passmak"[24].

You all are dissatisfied with our mediocre ambitions, and our "lɛh wi manaj am so[25]" attitude...you all rant on Facebook, WhatsApp..."all kine bactɔk...ɛn sing dɔn bɔs pan dis"[26].

Wetin du wi bah?
Why do we sabotage our best intentions?
Why do we intentionally, as Sierra Leoneans, take advantage of ourselves, our government, our wealth and revenue, our well-being? The soil beneath us oh, the air we breathe oh, the water we drink, oh, wi fine, fine beach dem oh!

Why do we sabotage well-placed projects, bleed them dry, discourage investors...discourage ourselves, settle and demand nothing more from each other than going through the motions...so, so book, wan sabi nɔr de de[27].

Is this country ours, or is it by some design, the providence of the UK, the World Bank, the US, China and the EU?
Because, I don't know about you, but our attitude to Sierra Leone is that, its wealth, institutions and future are not ours to build, invest in and preserve, but to fleece, pocket and destroy...make deal, ɛn go Dubai.

Yes, yes...each successive government can boast of a road there or here, education incentives here and there, a smattering of institutions barely breathing but alive, filled with square peg, apparatchiks and functionaries today, green ones, tomorrow red ones, next tumara[28], orange ones...all kolor ɛn im masta[29]...duplication, upon duplication.

My goodness, we are a nation of lack and we manifest that abundantly...unable to see beyond north or south, beyond those praise singers...achingly colourblind to competence.

Yes, yes, we had the rebel war, we had Ebola...we had a rundown of iron ore prices etc., etc...all these excuses to do anything but succeed.

Wetin du wi bah?

Saloneman ay!
Aren't you tired of this, our condition? Aren't you ashamed of our inheritance and now, our legacy?

Wi sɔri
Tem dɔn dɔn pan ple ple[30].

Wetin du wi bah?

Tejan Kabbah, for all his perceived failings showed us the way...the way of inclusive patriotic governance...some may say he had no choice, as the responsibility was to build up a nation from scratch...brick by brick, restoring institutions and dignity that had been razed and trampled on...amputated, and disembowelled.

Ernest Koroma won handily over the heir apparent, Brewah. Never has so much promise and charisma been squandered to stroke egos, seduce Brazilian-hair-wearing pokitos and bankroll, lavish lifestyles.

He hit the jackpot, walking into a country with plenty cash reserves...unspent and accumulated by his predecessor, a notoriously, crabbit leader.

This fine Bwoi[31], all smiles, all good intent, found himself at Casino Leone, with the mining industry exploding and brown envelopes raining...kids in a candy store, they all were. That prosperity agenda promptly gave all macru[32].

Life was so sweet, that a constitutional amendment to grant a third spin of the die was contemplated. After you, nah you, bo!

Salon

24 Canoe at Fogbo Village

Enter the "by any means necessary boys", silenced into submission for 10 years, watching mansions sprouting on the Freetown hills and up north...big deals landing and peggy[33] boys and gals, cashing out...they watched in horror and disgust as the excesses multiplied out of control.

And now a few years on...worn down by Corona, sucking air through masks or oxygen tanks at 34[34], we wonder if those were hollow promises.

The direction seems so long ago…outdated and disingenuous, because now, the only perception we can cling onto, is the adage, "the more things change, the more they repeat themselves".

Wither Lion Mountain?

Wetin du wi all bah?

The casino cannot continue…it is broken.
It's really not winner-take-all politics; it may seem and feel so initially, but in the long run, when the die roll again, we will find the odds stacked against us and our nationhood.

Wither Lion Mountain?

25 Sierra Leone Stamp 2

Rest in Peace, Kim Sung Nyeon
I met you once, and you related stories of your life and work in Sierra Leone. You were proud of what you had achieved, creating jobs and caring about the welfare of your workers.
May Sierra Leone be forgiven.
We know not the depths and fragility of a man's soul.

We

We, children of a new nation
Born into self-determination
Born into the dreams and aspirations of many
Independent and Free
Give praise and thanks.

26 Makeni – Kabala Highway, 2021

We, children of a new nation…from Bonthe to Kabala
From Kenema to Kailahun
From Makeni to Kambia
From Freetown to Sefadu
From Lunsar to Bo to Waterloh
From every hill and valley
From every river and forest
We hail.

We, children of a new nation
On this day acknowledging
And celebrating our differences
Diverse cultures and tongues
Stand united.

We, children of a new nation
As we give thanks for the preservation of
Unity, Freedom and Justice
Promise this day, to generations unborn
That they will never again

Smell the sting of burning flesh
Hear the sharpness of spilt blood
See the silence of arms hacked off
Feel the tenderness of disembodied heads.

Never again.
Will our fathers and brothers witness
Lacerated wombs on display
Deflowering of our mothers and sisters
Pain unending…conscience ripped.

We, children of a new nation
Now seek forgiveness from each other
Always need comfort from each other
Desire each other's encouragement and support when we falter.

Let us pledge this day.
Fifty years forth from that singular moment
Independent and Free.

Salon

That
When the least among us is harmed
When the least among us is defiled
When the least among us is stamped down
We all will feel that pain.

27 Views to the Hills

We, children of a new nation
Let us pledge from this day forward
To always move our land and our people
Towards the highest fulfilment of our shared humanity

Responsibility to each other
Prosperity for all

One Nation
One People
One Destiny
One Sierra Leone.

Welfare Bill

There's a certain mentality to African inheritors of a parliamentary system, from Great Britain, the "motherland" country...it seems the trend for these commonwealth Africans is to create in that body and by law, a golden path to the end...see Kenya, Ghana, Nigeria and now, Salon.

This generation of professional politicians, and indeed, most of our citizens; decades removed from the raw dominance and humiliation of being colonial subjects
Far removed from existing as second-class citizens, with the same rights as dogs, cattle and sheep
Far removed from the trade union and military sacrifices of the 1940s, 50s and 60s, they all have developed an affinity and need of wealth through legalized theft of public funds.

Imagine, calling it a Welfare bill, and putting forward compensation and graft at the expense of the farmers, the teachers, military, housewives; all plain, tax-paying citizens. Look at the state of us...shambles.

Actually, ours being a donor-propped up state, means that funds granted to improve the welfare of the average citizen will now be used to enrich these elected public servants.
We, a so-called Republic, have morphed into a constitutional monarchy, with parliamentarians suddenly barons, lords and the landed gentry.

The blood and deaths of a few short years ago have taught us naught. It must be a celebration to make it to the House party, where they Buga[35] for five years, then exit, richly gorging on the desserts of office.

We are ass-backward in our thinking, and our supposed patriotism. Are we really Sierra Leoneans, or just humans existing like animals, each trying to get richer than the next, by any means necessary? Our new anthem then, must well be:

28 Sunrise over Mount Auroel, 2021

High we exalt thee, realm of such greed
Great is the love we have for fees
Firmly united
Never we stand
Fleecing the gains from our grandchildren's hands.
Blessings and Peace
We never shall own
Land that we rob
Poor Sierra Leone

What We Need

We don't need aspirants
Or flagbearers
Or a poda-poda driver
Or likewise
Their assistants
Or popular sycophants
Destined or ordained
To carry on as before.

We need country before colour, creed or party.
We need country before sara[36] and prayers and fasting.
We need Sierra Leoneans with compassion
With vision

To set the direction and desire and love for country
To transform
Our backward tendency
Our innate and primitive need to grovel, to accumulate, to beg, to covet and steal.

I need you, Citizen, to be that leader
Not complacent and praying for deliverance
I need you to come with ambition and dreams for country.
I need to know that you are willing to lay life and limb necessary to crystallize a true, new nation.
We need a nation, united
Hope for the masses, reignited
We need justice to prevail – cut out the cancer at the root
We need the law
We need organization of our thoughts and being
Respect for life and for each other, Citizen.

No more pandering to our ignorant muses

Lifting up the unenlightened and crass existences as badges of honour and respect...
We need honesty, hard work and goal setting
We need transparent and fair existence in this republic.

29 Freetown, View from Tengbe Town

Citizen, you and I need to change.

Let us, at once, acknowledge the rot that has become.
We, the inheritors of such beauty and bounty
have proven unworthy guardians.

Rise up, Sierra Leone
From the freedom peninsula
To the Wara-Wara hills
The Gola Forest
Down the Rokel,
The Great Scarcies
The Mano
The Moa
The Sewa.

We are no different due to geography and destination
There is no pre-ordained destiny
Stand up for what is right
Stand up for what is true, with integrity
We all need to put country and the generations unborn first.

Start small
Each one, lift one.
Each selfless contribution
An immeasurable significance

Sorely needed
For this poor and wretched
land and people

To reach their potential
Fully.

Kush

Dried leaves sprinkled and smoked
Desperate lungs inhale deeply, absorbing into brain
Fragments and particles of an African civilization
That greatness of culture
Reduced to ash with new meaning
Producing insanity, stupor and suspended reality.

So much promise destroyed
Youth with hopes dimmed and dashed
Seek solace and euphoria in brief madness
We see them all around us
Slow, motionless, erratic, damaged souls.

The rot has entered the nation proper
Soldiers, police, workers – all in trance

Giving wealth to well-placed and connected pushers
Selling the soul of country
Burying the future, erasing talents, cancelling occupations
Mortal man reduced to flesh
Without care, memory
Or conscience
Zombies in our midst.

Kush reigns supreme
Destroyer of lives and limb.

Alagba Dem[37], beware.

Prayer is not a cure.
That knock at midnight was unanswered.

It is too late now to dam the deluge and inferno
Of thousands more around the corner…in our compounds,
at all intersections of our existences.

30 Tokeh Beach

That sweet smoke will seep through and overwhelm our every
intention.

Killing
    Unconsciously
        Spreading
            Harm

Salon

31 Sunrise over the Cemetery Wall - Kingtom

32 Solitary Sunrise

Part 3 – Politricks

Oporto-nity

Have you heard
Of how paper and a few words
Signed and delivered
Can form an understanding
A memorandum
And become gold?

Have you heard about
Those honourable Africans
Who wield magic in green pens?

They are alchemists
Who within cabinet concurrence
Generate bounty.

Have you heard and seen
The flock of Oporto[38] dis-investors
Hailing from every desperate corner
Promising fantasy and development mirages
Poised to create and distribute wealth from nothing?

Dem Africans are waiting patiently for their share in brown envelopes.

Politricks

33 Sunset at Sussex Beach

Peshawar – Baga – Garissa – Anywhere, Planet Earth

What is it that compels us…humankind
Whether written, and considered sacred
Whether uttered, and considered…revelation
Whether proclaimed, and considered the Law?

What is it that moves our kindred souls
To value us, their mirror image
As fodder
For bullets and bombs
And blind anger?

What is it that inspires us, rational beings
To murder for fashion
To burn alive for effect
To behead for sport
Or to fly into a mountain, or building for attention…
To walk in and pull a trigger
In the name of righteousness
In the justification of Heaven and Paradise
For the establishment of belief on earth
Or for the fun of it?

What is it that drives the Divine in us
To act with such depravity
Knowing not love
Nor reason
Nor empathy
To become judge and God

Extinguishing life
Erasing light
Destroying innocence
And, at once, rendering us who survive

Politricks

By chance of location or time...or nothing?
Numb...grieving...angry...questioning
And in pain.

What is it that compels us so?

34 Distant Sunrise

Tongues Tied

Sitting here in Bamako
Cradle of past empire
Cultural centre
Of a proud and deep people.

If you close your eyes and listen
As we speak in official settings
We English, French and Portuguese Africans

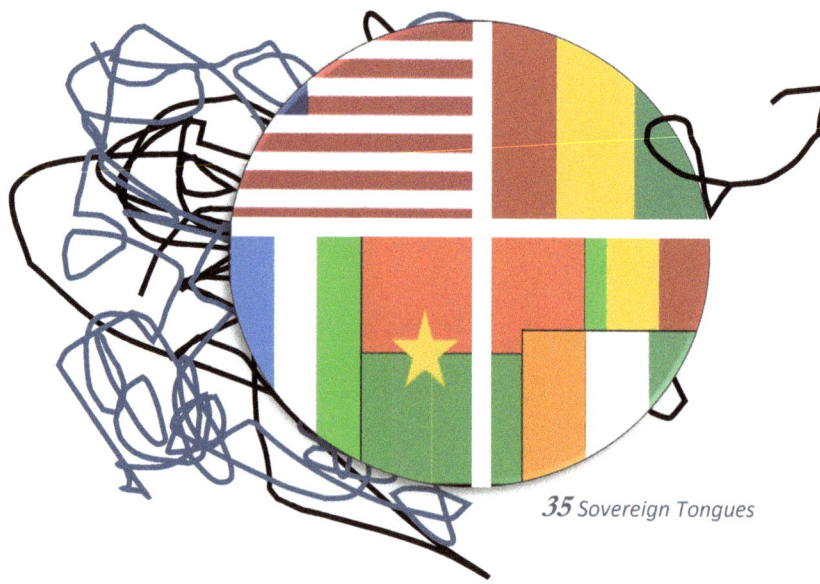

35 Sovereign Tongues

You realize that we have all inhaled the culture of the Seine,
the Thames, the Tagus, the Rhine and Potomac
Ignoring the majestic Niger, Mungo Park's "discovery"
Languidly flowing past in the distance.
Creations of brutal force and will, mapped with ruler and quill
in Berlin

Politricks

Shared after dinner desserts, really.
Served by white-gloved butlers.
The air perhaps tinged with swirling cigar smoke
Full scale monopoly with loaded die
Accumulation of territory
Instant divisions of people and places

Now proud nations
Each with allegiance, North and West
Tongues hewed and crafted to speak classically with perfect accent and attitude.

Even these words spilling on page
Fit snugly, like the black suits, Windsor collars and neckties of my compatriots
Sitting, politely discussing the future
Sweltering under the uncompromising Sun.

It's 96 degrees in the shade
But our thoughts are 180 degrees from Bambara, or Senoufou, or Malinke or Akan or Yoruba or Mende or Wolof or Fulbe

Alas
Tongues tied…in knots
Perfection created.

Power Trip

Power, and the need to hold onto it, is an intoxicating brew.
We really do not care so much about who said what, who posted what, who thinks what.

When the nakedness of ambition, combined with deep, unbounded corruption supersedes all promises of the New Path, and starts trampling on its own citizens

When the instability and inability of government is so visible…and felt throughout the land

When those in power start proactively looking at ways to remove checks and balances put in place for We, the People

When even within the venerated party, corruption is laid bare, and all rejoice in its outcome, reluctantly

When you conspire to illegally charge and remove leadership committed to this country, doing more for Brand Salon than most interventions over the last five years

We know then, that through all the bravado
Through the praise and worship of the co-opted masses, there is deep anxiety, a lack of self-confidence and an inability to deliver.

We need to desist from crushing legitimacy that threatens our self-confidence.
Instead, see how we can work with the others to make this Dunia[39] good for all of us, the people.

We love our peace and harmony in Salone. Leadership should transcend party politics and be able to secure and guarantee us that.

Politricks

It should stamp out any tendency from within government and party that seeks to divide us, create tension and further division.

Rise up to your oaths of office and always do what is right and just, for the benefit of generations hence.

36 CLSG Power Substation - Kenema

This is all we have – a piece of earth – on the coast of Africa, 300 miles from end to end...

Look gron good oh![40] Take heed.
So that friends, donors and governments that support and prop us up, will not wash their hands in disgust
Leaving us bare and rudderless.

Then again, we have never taken kindly to threats
Checkmate.

Wi Sɔri

Wi Sɔri
bak tɔk…ɛn siŋg dɔn bɔs pan dis…

Fɔgɛt ilɛkshɔn
Fɔgɛt simbɔl
Fɔgɛt kampen

Fɔgɛt Tolongbo dirɛkshɔn…
ɛn Paopa pila…

Fɔgɛt distrikt ɛn Prɔvins
Chifdɔm sɛf nɔ Mata
Fɔgɛt sosayti, fɔgɛt chɔch ɛn mɔsk…
Nɔ mɛmba yu vilej ɔ tɔŋg sɛf…
Fɔgɛt yu pipul ɛn yu pati
fɔgɛt ɔl dɛn dans ɛn muzik
We tin kam pan kam,
Na wi nɔ mɔ go lɛf na ya
Weteman nɔ gɛ fɔ sɛn shilin…
Ɔ kɔba klos fɔ wi.

Big wan dɛn unu yɛri o!
Tay di ɔja tayt.
Na Salon wi ɔl de
Ɛn dat nɔ gɛ fɔ chenj
Na wi yon don so,
Lɔnta…

.

Tweets and Vile Love Messages

In the stillness and chaos
One should no longer be surprised
By what comes out of the tweets
And from forked tongue, behind porcelain-capped rot
The vile language
Betraying the most visible agenda

37 Tweet Bird on Red with Star Bullet Holes

All our reaction and discussion
Feeds the putrid ego…
An insatiable hunger and obsession
With professed purity of race
And superior intellect

Without us, "the other"
Us the colourful
Us the compassionate
Us the love
Us the hue-mans
They will wilt

All their dislike
And hatred
An inadequacy
Made bare
Self-loathing, revealed
In its pure expression

Tweet away all day and night
Say all you want about our lack.
Deep down, you will always be lower
And can never rise above or buy
Decency and dignity.

Self-Evidents

Suddenly
Confusion
And fear
Take hold
So, too, the absurdity
The hate
And arrogance that have been
Brewing in the name of
MAGAnimity
Laid bare
Revealing the absolute putrid
Interiors.
Directionless, cowardice trying to sell and huck, rather than lead.

100 billion plus in armaments and escalating
Cannot soothe our beating hearts, anxious minds.
All of this is now, here and present.
In an instant, we have been rendered
Powerless.

In real time, we observe slow motion unstacking
Walls and guns are suddenly useless now.
We hold these self-evidents to be truths . . .

Empathy

Concern

Love

Are all we always needed.

Forgiveness

With impunity, violence and lies

Let us deify the godless

Let us transgress the constitution

Let us, blind to his acts

To the coded violence in his tweets

From his nepotism

For treasonous incitement

Think him still a saviour come

Born of virgin wealth

Marvellous king of queens.

Father, son and holy grifter

Injustice and hypocrisy without end

Amen.

Politricks

38 Bod Ose - Pademba Road and Bathurst Street

Settlers

Still a Colony
Even after 1961
Such a pity
With educated and erudite
Politicians and parties treating government as such
The tribe is a badge of honour in this arrangement
An anti-intellectual, "you nah weteman" pogrom.

A country under political spell of a party
Occupying offices with the mentality of colonial settlers
From the south, east, west or north
Ruling over us, the less fortunate citizen-subjects
In a winner-take-all governance.

A five-year colony for
Exploitation of country
Enrichment of tribesmen
Always cumulating with cosmetic projects to secure votes
Like clockwork, every sixty months.

Titles like Honourable, Director, Chairman and Excellency flourish
Securing a veneer of respectability and integrity
Cloaking deals and shady investors
A dime a dozen.

Since April 27, 1961
Extractive industry
Narrow, uninspired mind-set of lack
Rules our every waking moment.

Politricks

39 George Street House

Being Radical in Dreams Guarantees Everything?

Six lanes from Tagrin to Kissy
Driving from dream to reality
Holds promise of an economic miracle
For 8 million Africans eking it out in desperation.
It is decreed that we will suddenly become like Dubai
Moving goods, generating ideas
Inventing the future
Connecting the Futa Jalon to the bay of Benin
No bankroll needed
Just a concession of ores and land to fund.

Six lanes from Aberdeen, past Sawpit…connecting at ferry junction
The miracle mile
Hem the freedom city in
Disembowel all those panbodies[41] at the edge.

Gentrify, electrify and pacify the hungry
One billion, no two billion stars in our galaxy
And cars from sunup to sundown for miles
Will toll under cosmic rays.

New Leones converting to dollars and rubble
Big dreams are so alluring
Free things always priceless
Buyers of visions, beware.
Being Radical in Dreams Grant's Elections only.

Politricks

40 King Jimmy Harbour

Skin Deep

A paradox ain't it
Power and supremacy direct beauty
Bleaching skin, straightening hair
With nasal accented
Saviour dependency
Alleluia tongue-speaking
Dipping blackened sins in Jordan
Emerging white-as-snow in salvation

After 400 years of solitude
Negritude evaporates in a TikTok pixel.
Trying so hard to fit a jigsaw piece
In the wrong puzzle

And still in power, through digital influencers
Creating mirror images with
Plumped lips and tans
Butt-lifted cheekbones

Sometimes braids
Twang and slang
Rapping like Westside G's.

We circle each other
Warily
Trying to make it work out
But odds are stacked against

Politricks

The peso wall
And there's MAGA worship
In all places and continents
Grabbing pussies by the bushel

Resist the lull to slumber
Sharpen your vision
Adjust your existence
Remember the sacrifice
In blood and sweat.

Ancestors be praised
And exalted.

41 Red Grass Flower - Port Loko

Window Fragment

Almost 30 years ago
The bullet came clean through the window in my Mother's room
High up on the third floor.

Those were hell-on-earth days
Where tweens and Sobels[42] high on cocaine
Roamed the city
On a rampage from Foday.

Where bloodstained short-sleeved shirts
And unisex shorts
Were fashioned, hacked
To send a message:
Peace before election
As such
Cut hands couldn't vote
Cut legs couldn't run for office.

Thanks to Ecomog[43] lives and sacrifices
Lome negotiations
Sanity and peace prevailed long ago
And those toddlers are reformed citizens now.

For some reason, Mother never replaced the window
And almost 30 years since that bullet sliced through glass
High up
I still preserve this reminder
Monument to a time of shattered humanity.

Politricks

42 Bullet Hole through Window

My Brother's Keeper

There's an ugliness…unbecoming…threatening
Afraid really of my brother's ear
Said with such gravity and intent
No longer can they question or comment on the mundane.

My brothers
Natural leaders, go-getters.
You suddenly reject their hand…but what have you done
What plans have you made
To show appreciation and love?

You cannot be so insecure.
My brother knows my plight
And heaven knows they want what is best for us, equally without measure.
No dinner, or celebration is worth such aggravation and violence.

You cannot believe the compassion they have for you
The understanding and love
Of your many vulnerabilities
My brothers, who plan constantly to help you defeat the demons.

But how can you remove inertia from such mass
Create movement and need
Create desire in existence that is so calculated
Risk averse
Conservative
Self-sabotaging
Such promise and brain
Laying waste
Flapping in the wind as the years slip by.

Politricks

43 Royal Post Box – Hennessey Street, Kingtom

Hands Off Our Tree Campaign

Free menstrual pads to soak up the blood of the Ancestors.

Rape is not only physical
But through words and actions
Through indifference and purposeful ignorance
Harbouring hatred with violence-loaded speech.

It is, in fact, transgression of the powerful over the meek and accommodating

Strutting, dancing gleefully, and claiming innocence while your fangs voraciously rejoice in the cowering, quivering mess on your plate

It is the vanity doctorates and accolades accumulated to at last show equivalence – no, rather disdain of the earned sweat, polished speech, reserved manner of your nemesis.

Hands off our tree, our heritage

Our character and integrity…our manner

Our simplicity

Our being

Our unarmed and wretched existence

Let us be.

Politricks

44 Cotton Tree Stump, Cloudy Day

Lɛ I Pwɛl [44]

Is Freetown your capital city?

Yes, but lɛ I pwɛl

Is Freetown not part of Sierra Leone?

Yes, but lɛ I pwɛl

Is the Mayor doing her best for the city?

But nah ooman, Lɛ I pwɛl

en di clos we I wɛr, so, so rɛd…Lɛ I pwɛl

I! na so nɔmɔ?

Yes, dɛn too fityai

Lɛ I pwɛl

Politricks

45 *Pultney Street - Towards Bay*

Unrequited Love

I fell in love with her
This small, beautiful woman
Who promised to transform my life, give me direction and meaning

She came bearing palm fronds in her hair, intoxicating fragrance
And deep, penetrating eyes…dazzling and hypnotic.

She whispered softly, caressing each limb with urgent desire
With confident embrace, I dissolved into her depths
Pouted full lips and hips
Veiled and alluring
She broke all my defences.

And I, the strong and resolute, felt weak…my knees buckled
My heart afire
And I believed in her without reserve.

But reader, you know the rest.
I am bound with cut tongue, denied access, movement, free speech and thought.
Her kin have manifested dis-order, dis-unity and loathing through our land.
Somehow deep buried resentment has surfaced, buoying violently as the waves of the impending storm crash along the surety of our lives.

Incredibly, that beauty I once fell for, whole soul aflame
Has evaporated…laying bare
A vacuum.
Sanitized emptiness
No vision…just a flailing ember
Tossed about in every direction
Flying privately, dancing publicly, and mocking openly

Politricks

No plan or destination in sight.

There is no redemption to hope for, as the law is tossed aside
As protests and insurrection are conflated.
Accidents become assassinations…with language and media now propagating convenient narratives.
Rendering our sons and daughters restless…our elders, clutching their gnawing stomachs

46 *Water Pressure – Patton Street*

Disappointment is a disservice to describe the reality.
We are shambles…at the cusp of an eruption beyond measure on the richness scale.

We desperately need a natural mystic to reassure, rebalance and sooth these festering wounds.

We need dialogue
Forgiveness
Approval
Space
Tolerance.

I fell in love with her
This small, beautiful woman
Who promised to transform my life.
Please someone, anyone
Re-center her soul
Help her regain balance and strength
Let her know of our suffering
Tell her that in spite of her misleading direction
There's still a spark, and time
To be whole again…in love.

47 Sierra Leone Stamp 3

Section Two

Soil, Roots and Trunk

Part 1 – Fragility

Dust and Bone

When I pass
And transition over
I want you to acknowledge the wisdom and simplicity that Islam has shown us.

Wash the body carefully
Thanking God for the gift of life
Now returned to source.

Then, simply wrap in muslin
Tucking all corners with love
Let me face the sun in remembrance and gratitude.
No laying out for gawking and grief.

Then,
After prayer and thanksgiving for providence
In a fresh opening of the earth
Lay me gently down
No coffin or casket or vessel for the
corporeal journey.

I return to our Mother in communion, to celebrate the miracle of conception
Let the shell and bone settle to dust…naturally.

May the Almighty be exalted
Life and love without end
Amen.

Fragility

48 Dad. Ascension Cemetery

Have You Ever?

Oh!

Have you ever

Been so loved

When your son smiles at you

For nothing, except that you are

And runs into your arms for a hug

And simply says

"Hi Daddy."

Oh!

Have you ever

Been so loved?

Rest in Peace, Jamal

A Kingdom based on the sacred revelations…words holy to guide the soul

Suddenly afraid of what Jamal has said, has to say, will say.

100 million greens in the balance

I don't want to get into his mind

I mean, who knows…

Maybe they could be

Rogue Killers

100 million greenbacks can make you turn on a dime

Terrorists, hacking the internet or

Chopping bone

100 million greens spill out, splatter even

Our Red States of mind

See how the story and our minds have changed

Only God knows…Allah will judge us all.

Rest in Peace.

Are There Trees in Heaven?

Are there trees in Heaven?
Birds, whales, mosquitoes
Clouds, rain, rainbows
Thunder and lightning
Magnificent vistas

49 Sun-Flower Sketch

Are there bad hair days?
With sublime sunsets
Magnificent snowstorms

Fragility

Does palm wine exist?
And the need for memories cease
In that infinite existence of bliss and surrender

Will fireflies enchant us ageless souls?
And will all the untold mysteries unfold?

These I ask, for if heaven is another earth in a distant dimension, I can then believe, that my Mother and Father, and their parents stretching to the singularity

Will be there to love and embrace us.

For I would want in heaven
To feel Mother's warm envelope
Soak in her fragrance
To embrace Father, and all our past friends

I would like to hear the bad jokes, the long-winded stories of adventure

And surely, I would want to finally secure forgiveness for wrongs and sleights.

Is there a conscious self in Heaven
Or do all things physical die
To be reborn as part of the infinite whole?

Is there Heaven in Heaven, or is our existence here, perfection and manifestation of life's unending miracle?

50 Wild Flower – Moyamba, September 2022

Certainty

Indeed
We know not the day, the hour or the manner
But it is the single certainty of our lives.

So, let us appreciate while we can
With friends and family

The miracles many
The laughter and joy
The awesome glory and experience
Through the journey

Of this brief interlude.

51 Buried Cannon - Wallace Johnson/Gloucester Streets

Return

Such is life
At once joyful
At once sorrowful
So fleeting
Each day a treasure
Each friendship a happenstance
Each heartbeat a miracle
A sunrise is never guaranteed

We are but flesh and bone and thought
To Allah you return
May your path be clear

Rest in Peace.

Resting Place

Cemeteries in this city are a direct reflection of how we live;
Lack of self-love, dignity and respect for place is evident
No walls, no gates, no paths, no order, no plan
Just some ragamuffins in charge, scamming the JCs[45] and the living
Us with sɔiart,[46] grieving
Everyone land grabs and holds on for dear life.

These days
Final rites and prayers are prelude to disfiguring caskets;
Puncturing holes with sledge hammers and pick axes
Better to render them imperfect for re-sale or barter.

Then the vault packed with earth, wreaths, tears and regrets
Is sealed with a slab
Witnessed by family till the concrete dries

Someday
When the generations dwindle and the memories dry up
That grave, that space, will cave in
And another will be interred, six feet below
To Rest in Peace…for a while
Amidst the "Friends of the Dead[47]" incessantly claiming…
"Yu Bɔbɔ de[48]".

But not before the weathered bones of the previous occupants are gathered…tied neatly in a bundle, and placed in a far corner of the hollow.

Fragility

52 Circular Road Cemetery

Loss

Lost an acquaintance today.
And here I am,
Listening to octogenarians
Speaking Krio…reminiscing about life 40 years ago
Making lewd double entendres.

Acknowledging their frailty
Their mortality
Laughing about life's improbable coincidences
Its contradictions and minor miracles
Blue pills and mirth
Oh, what a life!

Tears in my eyes
Drowning in a delicious
Glass of wine
Life is good
But oh, so unpredictable.

Cheers.

Fragility

53 Wild Flowers – Ridgewood, NJ

54 *Plaque - Governor's Gate - Wallace Johnson Street*

Commander

Chale[49]

Is this the old age that we spoke of so sparingly in youth?

We were not to fall down so soon in this marathon

We were to go on…rejoicing in each other's milestones as the years add on
As the aches and pains take over.

We were to end up 25 years on
Drinking Scotch, talking trash
Dreaming about choristers and conquests, vividly existing, living fully.

We were supposed to fade out slowly with a smile on our faces
Love in our hearts…and souls on fire
Alas
Cut down, much too soon
Such is life.

Gone in a flash
But you mattered to each one of us, beyond measure.

Insomnia

Sleep is so overrated
With your mind and heart continuously racing
To get ahead of the heartache and loss
When promises and certainty are bludgeoned with steel rod
Flesh and bone are no match for the inertia and density of violence.

Gone too soon…head bashed in
Unrecognizable in the coffin.
And here he lies, motionless
As mosquitoes filled with blood buzz around.

Your revenge is not satisfying, but the bloodstained walls of the apartment mark the sure aim of the folded magazine.

You wonder what kind of life
What kind of future for that three-year-old, who speaks in complete English sentences.
Premature at birth, and so fragile
Curious and inquisitive now, with questions beyond his years.

Here he sleeps, snoring quietly, protected from all harm,
Loved beyond measure.

Sleep for me is so overrated
But the love of my life, my firstborn
Can slumber and dream on.

May the blessings never cease
May His Love provide guidance perpetually

Rest in Peace, Sholade.

Fragility

55 House on Charles Street

Wi Yon Pɔrsin[50]

Kam si sɛns and digniti
Kam si blɔf ɛn ajo
Kam si stratijist
Kam si bɔi pikin
Kam si ɔparetɔ
Kam si swit mɔt
Kam si mami blɛsin
Kam si sho bɔi
Kam si prawd Dad
Kam si aw man gɛt pɔrsin na bɔdi
Kam si aw wi kɔmpin ebul ɛp ɔl man wit doneshɔn ɛn lɔv

I nɔ gɛt mek mek…ɛn I sabi tɔk to pɔsin, bad bad, wan.

Ɛni bɔdi wɛ mit am, no se na spɛshal pɔsin ɛn gud mɔtalman

Wi tell Papa Gɔd tɛnki fɔh aw i blɛs wi wit am.

HM wi miss yu bo!

Fragility

56 Bai Bureh Ferry at Government Wharf

Sharpness

Oh Mother
For a brief moment
I missed you
Again.

That's life I guess
The pain dulls each passing minute
But there are moments

When the ground gives in

And you feel the rush of wind
As you flail…trying to regain balance.

Each day since
An After Mother, A.M. event
A tender, dew-filled dawn
An earth setting mourning, with the constant sun
In the horizon.

In gratitude, we say…
Glory be to our Mothers
And to the Sun
And to the Holy Universe
As it was in the beginning
Now, and evermore shall be
World without end.

And so, shall it be

Amen.

Fragility

57 Mother's Memorial Wreath

58 Ston Ose - Opposite Krootown Road Market

Part 2 - Gratitude

Give Thanks

Another year unfolds
And we celebrate in varying states
That moment…when light, sound and smell become manifest.
That day, when our entry is marked by a breath, then a cry
A cutting of the cord…and the incessant, beautiful sound of
a new-born voice.

We give thanks and praise for life
For our Mothers and Fathers – their Mothers and Fathers,
Ancestors on
For that link to who we are, past and present

We give thanks and praise for our siblings, who mirror us in many ways.
We give thanks and praise for our families, who deepen our definition of self.

We give thanks and praise to our friends…old and new…brief or long-lasting, who provide us with tapestries that give witness to the richness of living.

We give thanks and praise to the constant universe…the ever-rising sun, and the wonder of the moon and stars.

Another year unfolds, and we give thanks and praise to all-in-one, one-in-all.

Everlasting.

Gratitude

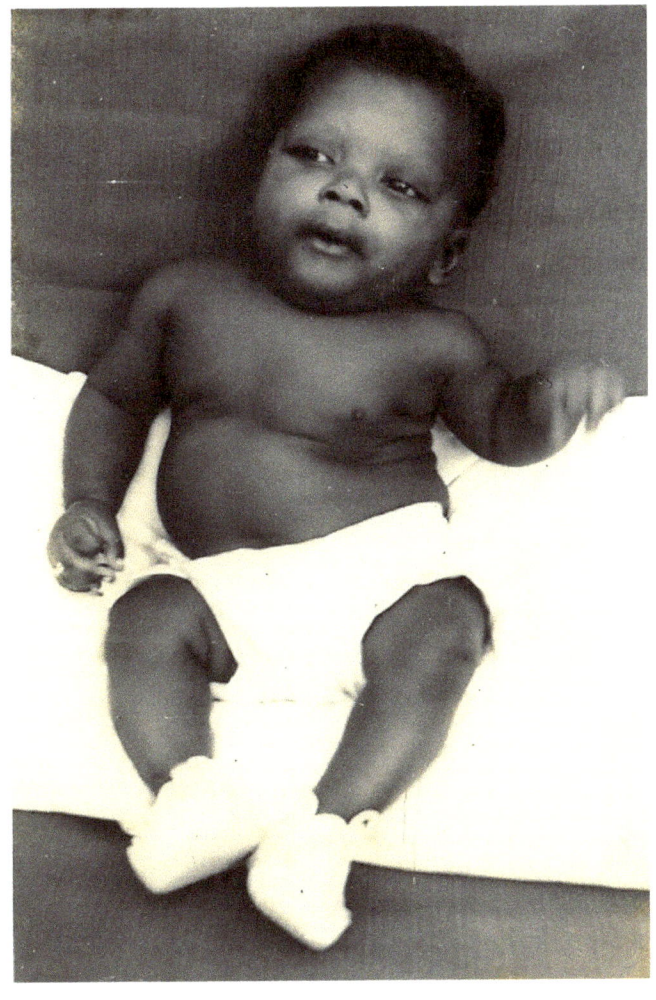

59 Baby C, 3 or 4 Months Old, 1962

A New Year Starts Every Day...

I suppose that a New Year starts every day
And depends on one's perspective

So, through loss and grief, anger and quarrel
Failure and despair
Through new birth and beginning, love and joy
Small victories and inner peace
Bridges, and crossroads to new directions
The New Year starts every day.

Open to endless possibilities
Stopping to breathe in
And sometimes to exhale
You suddenly realize that – Life is.

The sun will rise despite it all
The moon will go through its phases
Rain will fall and nourish the earth
Seeds will take root
Trees and flowers will bloom…bearing fruit
Birds will fly
And waves will continue to kiss the shore
All these will happen, life without end

A New Year starts every day.
And gives us pause to remember and acknowledge
All who have transitioned

Grief will fade
Our tears will dry up

Gratitude

60 Hibiscus - Aqua Club, 2022

And we will thank the universe
For creating the conscious us
Experiencing the beauty, the pain, the love all at once
Life is.

A New Year starts every day
And oh, what a sunrise to behold!

Dear Grandma

Just a little note to let you know, that we miss you so
Every day, we take pause to remember and give thanks
For all that you provided for us.

Starting with a coal pot to bake bread for your six, then seven children
You have given us wisdom to live by
Life, liberty, the love of learning
And words that still guide us today
"Envy no man. . .", "you go soba[51]. . ."

You taught us to be humble, and yet to be fierce and protective of family
In many ways, you blazed the trail
Independent, freethinker, resolute, quick-minded

We still miss the Christmas pudding, delicious cakes,
And the ginger beer

Today, anniversary of your birth, we pause and give thanks to the legacy that is Red Lion
We pause and give thanks for Family
'da rop we de bɛn, bɔt nɔ go brok[52]'.

We are eternally indebted to your example of hard work, sacrifice and unparalleled generosity that directs us, the generations expanding

Thank you….Thank you….Thank You….

Ethel Ashwood– 100 – Not out!

Gratitude

61 Ethel Matilda Ashwood - nee, Malamah-Thomas,
27 September 1913 – 26 September 1988

Dear Aunty Hawa

You were a real presence
A real person
Who always stood up for the right thing.
You were unafraid, bold.

As you have transitioned to the place of the Ancestors
We should crave your forgiveness
For our indifference
For our turning away.

We say it often
"Life is short…"
But until someone we know departs
Those words have no personal meaning.
Our time here is indeed fleeting.

But we are comforted, as perhaps is your immediate family
That your pain and suffering are over.
Without a doubt, you were dedicated in your work
A true civil servant
Whose service made a difference in the lives of your
co-workers, and the citizens we all serve.

Spirits do not rest
They live on eternally
So, for that brief moment
That the circumstances of life brought us together

We are thankful
ndig-ge ya-ha-lu[53]

Greet all those in the other realm
Stay true and blessed.

Gratitude

62 Traditional Gazebo - Tiama

In Awe of the Night Sky

We are relatively motionless
Above the clouds
The engines below
Roaring
The cabin lights all dimmed.

I look out
Beholding infinite stars, pin pricks of light littering the dark sky
Millions of constellations
A wondrous vista of
Distant suns of life
Each suspended in majestic impossibility
Through visible and invisible spectrums

Our Creator be praised
As is the sky above
So is the sky below
As is life inside
So is life outside
All through Infinite everlasting wisdom
Beyond our understanding.

We give pause and praise
Eternal gratitude
For this engagement
All of us so brief
Insignificant flashes
In flesh
Acknowledging when we can
The awesome tapestry.

Gratitude

63 Full Moon. Freetown, 2020

With Humility and Gratitude

For all the goodness and blessings
For the untold generosity and sacrifices of Ancestors known and unknown...for the care and love of Great-Grandparents, Grand Aunts, Grand Uncles

For the support base village of Aunts, Uncles and relatives who continue to shower me with wisdom, direction and elevation

For the continuous care and appreciation of my Cousins, their Families...Nieces and Nephews...my adopted Families in North Carolina, Texas, New Jersey, New York, the UK, Freetown, Accra and more

In loving memory of my Grandparents, Parents and Parents-in-Law...Mammy Adah, Grandpa Cyril, Pamela, Cyril
Olive and Ransford

For the unquestionable joy...of my Brother, Bryan, and Sister, Desiree, who always have my back

For newly formed and lifelong friendships

For classmates of 55+ years ago: Ausora, College School, Prince of Wales School...and the indelible brotherhood of PRESEC and the 1979 year

For those years at Temple and Pratt universities

For the thousand and more colleagues: New York, London, Freetown and in-between...all those who have given me a chance, a dream and a belief in my abilities, to work and serve

Gratitude

For all the circumstances of life that continue to bring people, places and experiences into my orbit…with the never-ending support and selfless love of my Wife and Sons

64 Sussex Beach, 2021

Six decades and counting

Thank You

Thank You

Thank You

Regional Power

In memory of Mansa Musa and his empire
In memory of all the Ancestors and their wisdom
Stretching from the banks of the Nile to the Ethiopian highlands

Across the sands of the Sahara
Winding through the rich forests that fostered our livelihoods
and civilizations
From Nubia and Sudan and the fertile rift valley of the East
With its majestic mountains and swooping valleys of tea terraces

To Table Mountain and the ores of gold, rivers of diamonds South,
to the coltan and copper veins of the Congo
The deep oil and gas in the Niger Delta, running along miles of
coasts to the Kalahari

To the red laterite soils, with palm, cocoa and coffee
Bananas, yam and cassava
To the memory, more recent of Houphouet-Boigny, Nkrumah,
Senghor, Nassar, Toure, Tubman, Margai…and their current heirs
To the millions of mothers who bore us…and raised us silently

Today, we raise our glasses to pour libation to the earth that holds
your bones and memories.
We thank you for this time in our lives.

This special moment, where a spark of energy, can run from Man in
Cote D'ivoire, to Monrovia and Mano in Liberia, to Kenema,
Bekonghor, Bumbuna, Yiben and Kamakiwe in Sierra Leone, to
Linsan in Guinea and all the towns and villages on its path

Gratitude

A prelude of a bright future to come for all our citizens.

Indeed, the dream has been realized and now, it is up to us to ensure its survival far into the future.

Today, that spark of energy will travel thousands of miles, connecting us as one people, for generations to come.

DrRandomFactor, CC BY-SA 3.0 <https://creativecommons.org/licenses/by-sa/3.0>, via Wikimedia Commons

65 Africa - Colonial Dessert

Friendship

There's really a dimension to us that have chosen to brave the rain and murk
The frustration and uncertainty of every day.
We yearn for days of our youth when
Without a care
We knew we were invincible
And that our parents, with all their follies and faults, would live forever
Time was suspended in this our Eden - Idyllic.

To be back here…witnessing one-by-one, as those who raised us return to the earth and memory
As this country sinks in deeper to directionless poverty
And paucity of mind and vision

It's our friends who show love
Our friends who delight in us
Our friends with whom we fight
Sometimes dislike
That prop us up
And keep us going.

Things will never be the same
Age creeps in
Our memories fail

But my loves, thank you
For being and caring
For the small and big celebrations
That enable and connect us.

Gratitude

Let us enjoy ourselves.
With music
Dance
Good wine

Sweet stories
Great quarrels
And gut-filling laughter.

Amen.

66 Night Lights over Freetown, 2022

Instruction Manuals

Instruction manuals are necessary to understand...to set up and build.
They give comfort in knowing the sequences and outcome of process for complex machines
Or situations encountered in life.

Not so with birth
From the moment the crowned head emerges...with placenta and primordial fluid
The first cry...the cut cord
Linking mother to child...a continuum, from the Source.

There are no instruction manuals to predict, prepare and provide
As the universe entrusts you with a new life, the enormity of responsibility sprouts
No nurses to guide
No doctors to reassure.
There are no instruction manuals to prepare you for the colic and cries, round-the-clock fatigue, sleepless stupor of diaper changes, furious feedings and endless worry.

There are no instruction manuals provided, but with the counsel of grandparents, extended family and friends
As you survive and make it through that first month, first six months, first year
The pieces and parts slowly emerge, engage as necessary
Growing and blooming this miracle of life
In your trust for a lifetime.

No instructions indeed
As each page and chapter unfolds.

Gratitude

67 Yellow Bell - Maroon Church Yard

68 Cathedral House

Part 3 – Nostalgia

EJE

There are some memories
Deep in childhood
Sweet.

My grandfather holding court at 29 Westmoreland Street
With constant Black Label and soda
And all those stalwart Grandmen...
Galba-Bright, Uncle JB, John Mala, Uncle Pelu, Uncle John, Uncle Herbert, Maurice Jones...occasionally, Everet Gooding, Doc Jones, HEB John, Ned John, Ernest Auber, Justice Brown-Marke, Walter Nicol Snr, Nelson Ashwood . . . all gone now.

It was ten shillings for the JP signature and seal...a pound for a certified oath.
Leones? What were those?
And weekly, those Littlewood Pools form entries, with promise of a win, got ticked and packaged and sent to London!!

My grandfather, I must confess, spoiled me rotten with bags of Natco toffee, diamint...and a share of his lunch. Usually rice and stew or Bwel Soup[54]...definitely NO Plasas![55]

Those were heady days...at 1:30 p.m., the bus from Fourah Bay College School would drop us up at Tower Hill
Then I would make my way past that garage school, and the municipal one...past the sentried gate at statehouse, walking towards the grandeur of the Cotton Tree

And there, with our front-row view of the law courts, was his office. He sat at that mahogany desk, with its high front of cubbies and slots for paper, paper clips, wax seal, rubber stamps and all sorts of keys....

Nostalgia

Typing quickly with one finger
He provided a service, for certification and proof of documents
As a Justice of the Peace
Efficient and brusque

The air was rich with the vapours of Johnny Walker and the occasional cigar.

69 Eustace Josephus Ekundayo Ashwood, 1898 - 1974

A Gentleman's haven...
With banter and laughter and raucous teasing all day
Then I would get my 20 cents and run to the Kortoh[56] next door,
sometimes to buy a biscuit or two.

In those days, George and Trelawney Streets were lined with trees and shade.
My grandfather was my shade; he was larger than life...tall and regal,

Unafraid and yes, prickly.

How many have had the honour of helping a grandparent wash and dress?
His shirts were starched, with interchangeable collars…wool pants with proper cuffs, white underwear, suspenders
I still remember the stiches running down his hip. The surgery left him with difficult mobility.

But he possessed a lively wit, natural charm…and an agile mind.

Once a month or so, we would clean his rifle, with oil and cloth….and I, as an eight-year-old, knew where the bullets were.
He would sit, load the gun and aim at the vultures sitting on the electric cable across the street
Cursing loudly, if he missed…trespassers, beware!

He was impatient, a trait we all share…intemperate for any waste of time.
My grandfather, a self-made man…a police officer…a grand-master of the brotherhood
Confident and driven.

I remember those days, toasting the New Year with champagne…the family whole…the generations spreading, the sons and daughters, all tall and funny and alive…Red-Blooded Lions of the Pride.

Rest in Peace, Granddad.

With gratitude and love…

Baby C.

Nostalgia

70 Red Lion through Window - Kingtom

Inspired

Growing up, I was surrounded by strong, independent women. Women who got up every day and worked...with passion and creativity.

My Mother, Aunts and Grandmother - each one, with the responsibilities of motherhood - made their way and mark in the world, but more importantly, their ferocious love, their no-nonsense attitude, with large doses of humour, wit and sarcasm, moulded my worldview.

As modern women in the late 20th Century, specifically Krio women, they hailed from a tradition that values education and contribution to society.

What we take for granted was, and really is. not the normal path and life for millions of women around the world.

71 Ashwood Family, 1952

Yesterday was the 230th anniversary of the founding of Freetown and its unique Krio culture...and I learned that Krio women were the first to vote in the world as Head of Household, long before the suffragette movement took hold and won the universal right. Believe!

As a young boy, our extended family household was headed by women...my Grandmother Ethel, first to pass the Cambridge entrance exam in Sierra Leone, mother of seven, entrepreneur

Nostalgia

extraordinaire, founder of Red Lion Bakery.
My Mother, Pamela a teacher and raconteur, who could hold court with spellbinding stories and jokes...but don't dare get on her bad side...

My Aunt Gloria, the first female Chief Librarian of Sierra Leone, to whom I owe a love of reading and classical music, and whose handwriting I have tried to copy.

She made sure she brought home books for us every week...she exemplifies the best of emotional intelligence and clarity of thought.

72 Adah Grant, nee Johnson

My Aunt Gracie, Madam Williams as many know her, indomitable former Headmistress of the Annie Walsh Memorial School – the oldest girls' school in West Africa. Sharp wit and intelligence.

My Aunt Jestina, a powerhouse athlete, teacher and business person...

With this background, every day was Women's Day.

Today, I also want to pay tribute to my paternal Grandmother, Adah, head of household, who raised five children. Baked and sold ginger cake, coconut cake and pepper mint on Krootown Road.

My Mother-in-Law, Olive, a double professional as a qualified nurse and an erudite lawyer, one of the first women to establish a law practice; Omopeleyin Chambers.

It really takes a village. So with gratitude, I salute the women in my life: our Ancestors, my Wife, Aunts, Cousins, Teachers, Godmothers, current and past Friends, Confidants, Connectors - today and every day for their loyalty, fight, love, sacrifice and that ethereal quality that is.

73 Gracie, Pamela, Jestina and Gloria - 1980's

Nostalgia

Salon Bred

Water, flour, yeast
Pinch of salt
The simplest of parts.
Mixed and kneaded
Weighed and divided
Each fold, turned on itself
Rolled oblong
Or rounded to a ball

Will rise.
Its skin, taut
With that familiar sheen
Carried on metal sheets and moulds
Glistening with oil.

Mangrove fire ablaze
Provides the necessary heat
Transforming, as the steam evaporates
Leaving crust outside and air pockets within.

Bread
Oven hot, just so, to melt Anchor butter
Or in my case, I remove the gut
Preferring, just like my Mother did
The crunch of crust
The familiar salty, yeasty flavours and smells
Inhaled at first bite

Born and Bred
Salon inheritance
Mixed and kneaded
Weighed and divided
Each fold, turned on itself.

74 Red Lion House, 1948 – 13 Bolling Street, Kingtom

Third generations are fragile.
Like bread, with simple ingredients
Water, flour, yeast, pinch of salt
Which can suddenly turn into mush
If not measured carefully
Or burn, if rendered too long
In the fire.

Nostalgia

As the years pile on, this pride of Lions has bruised through its share of fragility
As misunderstandings, sleights, sibling rivalries
Dis-inheritances and mistrust seep into the mix
A recipe for sourdough.

Words spoken cannot be recalled
But try we must, to rectify the slurry
Heal the cleavage riven as we rise
Since 1944
Three generations and expanding…

Water, flour, yeast…pinch of salt
The simplest of parts
Mixed and kneaded
Also needs love.

75 Salon Bred

76 Malamah House

Nostalgia

Vistas

Driving up to Hamilton
With my son, soon to turn
20
The same age I was when I
ventured across the Atlantic
40 years ago.

Bright eyed, ambitious,
confident, green, with the
fresh-off-the-boat glow of
innocence, likely gained after
a most modern, shackle-free
middle passage.

To think that a century and a half before, that path, well-trodden, created wealth and woe on continents asunder with the Trade With the sweat and brow of melanin-hued gold.

And now, so many of us lured by the promise, myth and stories of Brand America…the dream, of which the Preacher spoke. Amerikkka, the anything-is-possible-and-achievable state of mind.

On arrival, the I-95 highway; the solid and sinewy ode to the

Amazon, Nile and Niger; full of cars and trucks, bore us

Winding its way from New York to the Carolinas in an awe-inspiring surge; connecting the crack strewn jungles and veins of the 1980's East Coast.
Six lanes whizzing through to the future.

Today, here we are, on a pastoral, two-lane county road keeping to the 35 mph limit, with snow covered vistas, both sides for miles;

We sail past desolate pine forests, and meadows stripped bare of foliage and fauna; hibernating till spring.

The hills around us are familiar.
Like those on the edges of
Freetown; graceful, rolling, languid lions resting.
Memories are triggered…as we pass abandoned farmsteads, with
sprigs of cattle or grain dotting the horizon.

Nostalgia

The blur of bare forests, ghostly shed frames and grain towers are a poignant reminder of life's ebb and flow.

Everywhere there are thick, virulent tree trunks...standing upright and tall, surrounded by young saplings struggling to inch up.

And yet in their midst, are fallen trees also; broken, snapped. Rotting into the snow.

All is in perfect balance, as time stretches out omnidirectional
Each moment endless, but our presences that bear witness to the change before us, limited.
Praises for the sacrifices and love that propel us still...
Guiding and guarding our beings...
As the future opens up continually.

77 *Malamah House Interiors*

Nostalgia

78 Malamah House Staircase

Talking Trash

There's a video going round in mid-2022
Showing Japanese fans after a game at the World Cup in Qatar
Picking up debris and cleaning up.

It's not their job
They are not obligated or
Contracted to do so
But here they are
Gathering up the trash of long-gone
Exuberant fans.
They do not do this for Tik-Tok views
Or some other social media click

But profoundly as one of them says,
". . .because we respect the place."

Suddenly, it is clear
In Kigali, it's the same ethos…Rwandans have had their self-dignity restored.
It is such a clean and tidy city.

And so, it is with us humans…without respect for place

Without self-dignity to anchor
We defile, clutter, dump and live in the middle of a functioning landfill, overflowing with the detritus of our existence.

We need to reset
Re-evaluate
And redirect our energies
To restoring dignity and respect for each other
And the spaces we share.

Nostalgia

Our shared humanity and common decency
Requires decluttering
Continuously.

79 Washed Ashore - Lumley Beach

Addis Deities

It's high noon in Addis
And I've decided to take a break from sightseeing.
So, walking away from the main street
I look for the beer garden
Local enough to offer food that I crave
Lamb tips sautéed in onion and vegetables, eaten with
Injera…washed down with a cold beer.

We are seated outside, under the shade of a canopy, built to look like a traditional hut
And suddenly, six self-assured, gorgeous melanin goddesses
Every shade under the sun, arrive
My heart skips
If only I was four-decades younger…and, of course, single.

My Sons should be here, to enjoy the view and perhaps engage in the rapid-fire chatter; full of life and promise and future possibilities.

Oh, how they charged the convection under shadow, unaware of their power
Natural
Beautiful
Unburdened
Confident.

The future looks wonderful for this generation of African deities.

Nostalgia

80 Injera - Addis Ababa, March 2023

Marriage Is No Mirage

True to form
Marriage is no mirage
But on that day
With the exchange of vows and rings
Hearts afire

After the toasts, and dances, life takes over
Young loves aglow
Then, if you are lucky, start families, change jobs
Enter professions
Move cities
Buy cars
Buy or build houses
Pay bills.

I want you to know that I am grateful for your trust, patience and belief.
True to form, Marriage is no mirage.
We've had our moments and learned to clean up the spills
Mop the floors
Repair broken mirrors
Polish patina.

True to form, Marriage is no mirage.
It frames the milestones and sweet memories
The life of a home with growing children
Packed lunches
Piles of laundry
Soccer practice
Lacrosse kits
Bicycles
Game Cube and Wii consoles
Biddy Basketball tournaments

Nostalgia

81 November 4th 1961

Band instrument rental
Science fair projects
Incessant homework.
First, at the Montessori and kindergarten, then the primary school across the street
Graduating to Middle school, two blocks away
Then to High School, a 10-minute walk east
And now, out of state, to College

True to form, Marriage is no mirage, no suburban dream.
With it leaks, blocked toilets, expired light bulbs and replaced driveways
We recollect the continuous change of seasons
Glorious summers with barbecues, fairs and music concerts
Weekend soccer tournaments
Unruly lawns and hedges
Miles of hose and sprinklers
And by October, with its lengthening shadows
Pine needles and golden leaves fall, and fill the yard.

Then snow and wind take over
Ice sheets and 18-inch drifts on sidewalks to clear
Menacing trees swing and sway as snow ploughs hem us in
Packing the beautiful, picturesque flakes up against the fence
A constant battle digging out, chipping the freeze
Cursing loudly, each breath visible below zero.

In spring the melting waters give life, awaken the soil and latent bulbs push through, bursting forth to bloom.

Marriage is no mirage
Through these seasons
We have thrived
Fashioning a home and family.

Nostalgia

82 Variegated Hibiscus, 2012

83 The Suns - Football Stars

Nostalgia

For Those of Us with Black Suns

My Son...all 5 ft 8 of him...strong and beautiful...loving and considerate

He kisses me still, before bedtime...and hugs are never spared
He says, "I love you"
A boy still, and yet a man also.

Today, I want to envelope him and protect him from the elements.
From the dagger eyes...from the .38 and 9mm eyes...from the neighbourhood watch eyes
From all the eyes that do not know him...yet, condemn his being.

My Son, all short, nappy hair of him...all brown iris of him
I want to build concrete armour and a bulletproof mind canister for him to wear.

I want to buy a superhero button for him...one push, and he's not there...where he's not wanted.
One push, and he disappears, undoing the never-ending label of skin and fear and loathing.

My Son...the all-American-ness of him, all brilliant smile, smart-aleck, all basketball, all soccer, all texting, all TV, all Xbox...all hoodie and sneakers and Skittles, all candy and soda of him.

I want to buy him an army. No!...Special Forces with marine backup and drone protection, just for him...so he can wander and wonder freely.

Taking claim north, south, east and west, at the table and in all the spaces of this, our bountiful country.

Lεh Wi Pre

Mi fambul dεm we dɔn go bifo, we de opin road fɔ wi, fεt fɔ wi, εn mεn wi.

Duya unu kam tinap wit mi…pamεla εn ciril pikin…

Unu kam ol εn sho mi ow fɔ waka wit kol at εn Alafia…

Wi ɔl cɔmɔt na sem tik εn grɔn.
Wi ɔl nah sem nabul string, εn nah wan mami bɔn wi ɔl.

Unu de yeri we wi de beg wit sɔri at…
Unu dε si altin we de mɔna wi…
Unu nɔ lεf wi oh!

Lεh wi gεh welbodi εn ful pɔkit te go, fɔ lε wi go mεmba unu blεssin εn all di gud wɔke wi unu du na dis lif.

Ar nɔr fɔget mi prɔmis fɔ ol ɔp wi fambul nam tiday, tumara εn te go…

Unu tenki fɔ di blessin.

Nostalgia

84 Railway Bridge behind Gibraltar Church

Notes

Section One
Part 1 - Fritong

Freetown
Ode to a hometown with a difficult history. Hoping it will evolve to live up to the national tenet of "Freedom, Unity and Justice".

Flotilla
Imagining the journey over the Atlantic. Halifax to Freetown. 15 Ships, 1100 Hopeful Souls

Lush Green Canopy
Ode to the Cotton Tree, the totem of Freetown and its peoples. Reflection on the anti-government violence that erupted on August 10, 2022. Leading to the brutal deaths of five police officers and scores of unknown citizens.

Monuments and Relics
Another look at Freetown and history. Freetown as both a monument and a relic.

Rooted, Ruins and Resilience
Inspired during a ferry ride between Lungi Airport and Government Wharf. A beautiful day that revealed the history of the river, the bay and the resilience and determination that led to the founding of the first University in modern Africa.

Ekonomiks
An observation on transportation and employment. Especially poignant with rising cost of living and an explosion of the population.

The Orphanage, the Company and a Country
The transformation from liberation of 150,000 Africans to a republic today, of some seven million. The broken promised land of Unity, Freedom and Justice.

Transformation
Fading city with memories of its settlers and the streets that defined a well-ordered existence...

Notes

Ghosts
Writing on Freetown of the past that's slipping into history and irrelevance.

Futility
Freetown, a once beautiful, orderly city has been reduced to a dump. Despite its magnificent natural beauty, so sad to see its slide into a messy slum in all areas.

Crown Title
The issue of formerly protected Crown Lands, the unfair land tenure system and the grab for land in Freetown and the Western Area.

Broken, but Not Uprooted
Written a few days after a storm finally brought down the historic and beloved Cotton Tree in May 2023.

Part 2 – Salon

All is Not Lost
Written just before the 2018 general Elections in Sierra Leone.

In Dependence Day
Lucky to be at the State House on Sierra Leone's 60th Independence Day Celebrations, April 27, 2021.

Waetin Du Wi bah? (What Is Wrong with Us?)
Frustration at things Sierra Leone. Politeness, discourse, hygiene, transparency, merit, leadership, patriotism have all declined. Businessman Nyeon committed suicide after having his business destroyed by delays, ad-hoc regulations and fees, lack of timely approvals and demand for inordinate kickbacks by senior government officials at the Ministry of Fisheries.

We
Written on the Sierra Leone's 50th Independence Day Anniversary.

Welfare Bill
Parliament decided to push through a bill with increases in salaries and gratuities. This, in the middle of austere times for Sierra Leone.

What We Need
Written in 2017 during the height of the 2018 general elections campaign in Sierra Leone.

Kush
A drug-fueled scourge on the country with addicts of all ages and occupations, nodding off in a slow-motion death spiral. Cheap and available, it continues to destroy lives and livlehoods.

Part 3 – Politricks
Oporto-nity
The machinations of briefcase investors and projects, and the unspoken process to secure approvals and government buy-in.

Peshawar - Baga - Garissa - Anywhere, Planet Earth
A series of attacks in 2015: Bombing and suicide attack at a Shiite Mosque by the Taliban, killing 19, Al Shabab killing 148 people at Garrissa University, Kenya, and the Boko Haram Massacre on the North Eastern Nigerian Town of Baga.

Tongues Tied
A real moment of clarity in Bamako, Mali, while attending a regional Energy Summit…a clash of French and Anglo attitudes and accents among fellow Africans.

Power Trip
Power Corrupts….Absolute power corrupts absolutely. (Lord Acton)

Wi Sori (We Are Wretched)
A sad state of affairs to be citizens. No pride or ownership in our national destiny.

We Are Wretched (Translation)
With angry tongue and speech everywhere

Notes

The election doesn't matter
Your values and the campaign don't matter
Forget
And
It doesn't matter what district or province you come from
What Chiefdom even.

Your social club, your church and mosque are irrelevant
Likewise, your hometown or village
Your family and your party are insignificant
You will no longer dance and rejoice
For in the long run
We will remain
No one will come to save us with money
Or warm blankets.

Oh, wise people, listen
Be prepared
Sierra Leone is all we have
Forever, without change
We are doomed.
So be it.

Tweets and Vile Love Messages
The Tweeter-in-Chief inspired this one.

Self-Evidents
At the height of the COVID pandemic, we suddenly realized how powerless and vulnerable we humans are.

Forgiveness
Can one forgive the excesses of Donald Trump?

Settlers
Colonial Politics is still the same: Exclusive, extraction and enrichment.

Being Radical in Dreams Guarantees Everything?
Dreams and visions of a Wakanda-like, smart city, connected to Freetown across the mouth of the Rokel River by a proposed $2B BRIDGE. Dream or Reality?

Skin Deep
Standards of beauty have long been directed by whiteness...but now, co-opted African-ness is all the vogue.

Window Fragment
Civil war ravaged Sierra Leone in the 1990s with atrocities that shocked the whole world: Wanton rape, beheadings, burning of whole villages, civilians limbs amputated as a message to the Government. We must pledge that never again, will this happen.

My Brother's Keeper
African men, black men need protection from the predatory and unfair world at large.

Hands Off Our Tree Campaign
Sierra Leone has so much promise, but our politics and our politicians have only an enrichment agenda. A play off the country's "Hands Off Our Girls" campaign. We need a radical change of culture for progress. We need genuine empathy and transparency.

Le I Pwel
The apathy of its residents, in the sprawling metropolis, is appalling. The City is overrun. Lack of order, crumbling sanitation and the preponderance of tin shacks and street sellers indicates a deep seated social problem, that Central Government should help address.

Unrequited Love
A love affair gone wrong. The allure and the attraction have all vanished. We gave our all hoping for reciprocity, care and concern from our true love, Sierra Leone

Notes

Section Two
Part 1 – Fragility

Dust and Bone
There was a period, between 2017 and 2021, where I attended many funerals in Freetown.
I have always been wary about the expense, emphasis and extension of grief, the rituals and time of typical Christian funerals in Sierra Leone, compared to the simplicity and speed of Muslim burials.

Have You Ever?
This was written when my older Son was perhaps four or five years old. The simple love and trust. Good to reminisce.

Rest in Peace, Jamal
Jamal Kashoggi was brutally murdered. None of the Human Rights nations batted an eye lid. Then of course, the American President at the time…bruh! He kept on tweeting and apologizing on behalf of the Saudi.

Are There Trees in Heaven?
Another questioning of the Afterlife. Thinking especially of my Mother and Father even at 59+.

Certainty
Reflection on the fragility of life.

Return
On the loss of a friend, Ramzan, who passed away suddenly. Acknowledgment of the return to the Source.

Resting Place
Freetown cemeteries are a disaster. Chaotic and unorganized…similar to the lives and spaces inhabited by the living.

Loss
Late evening, out with friends and enjoying their company but still shaken by the loss.

Commander
Emmanuel Tetteh was a classmate and dorm-mate at PRESEC. A consummate gentleman who rose to become Head of the Ghana Border guards. Died suddenly of a heart attack in Accra.

Insomnia

My Mother would never sleep, and would walk around the apartment, folded magazine in hand, killing mosquitoes. I suppose the trauma of my Father's death was partly responsible for the worries and lack of sound sleep, even years later.

Wi Yon Pɔsin (Our Dear Friend)

Henry Olufemi Macauley. Ambassador of Sierra Leone to Nigeria, then Minister of Energy: 2014 to 2018. We worked side by side. Henry was a true leader, with brains, energy and superb emotional intelligence. His death was a big blow to me and his many friends and family. He was a Tour D 'force, gone much too soon.

Our Dear Friend (Translation)
Intelligent, dignified
Full of swagger and concern for others
Strategist....
A Gentleman's man
Smooth operator
With a gift of the gab
Blessed
Impeccable in bearing and manner
A proud father
If ever there was a caring person
Let me tell you about our dear friend
Generous and loving to all in need with donation and love
He was humble, and approachable
Anyone whose path crossed his can attest
Here is one special human being.
We thank God for his life
HM, you are truly missed.

Sharpness

In Remembrance of my Mother: 29 July 1934 to 13 March 2014…
Mom died three weeks before I returned to Freetown to start a consultancy as Project Manager, Bumbuna 2. It was a surreal experience that left me reeling. I had to delve headfirst into work in order to overcome the grief. Death of a mother, especially, is hard.

Notes

Part 2 – Gratitude

Give Thanks
Written on my 49th Birthday.

A New Year Starts Every Day...
New Year wishes 2015.

Dear Grandma
My maternal grandmother was a tour de force. Wriiten on her 100th birthday anniversary.

Dear Aunty Hawa
Hawa was a colleague at the Ministry of Energy. She suffered a stroke and died quite suddenly. However, she had been also treated unfairly during her term at work.

In Awe of the Night Sky
Really an awe-inspiring experience, flying from Accra to Nairobi at night.

With Humility and Gratitude
On the occasion of my 60th birthday (born September 7, 1962).

Regional Power
Cote D' Ivoire, Liberia, Sierra Leone, Guinea Transmission Project (CLSG) kicked off. This is a 1300 km line that runs from Cote D' Ivoire through Southeast Guinea, Liberia and Sierra Leone and finally terminating in Linsan in southwest Guinea. I was instrumental in contract negotiations on behalf of the government for energy and transmission contracts.

Friendship
Reflection on friendship among the few of us who have dared to return and remain in Sierra Leone.

Instruction Manuals
Reflection on birth and raising of children. What an experience and growth!.

Part 3 – Nostalgia
EJE
Nostalgia. Ode to my Grandfather's time and generation.

Inspired
For some reason, I got inspired on Mother's Day in 2022. Talking and texting to a support group of friends consisting mainly of Women, Aunts and Mothers, made me reflect on my Mother and the Women in my life village.

Salon Bred
Family ties, inheritance and the need for resolution and love.

Vistas
Right after Christmas, in early 2022, I had the privilege and bonding experience to drive my Son Kwame to College in Hamilton, New York. I spend most of the year away from my family, so this was a welcome and enjoyable trip.

Talking Trash
The need for restoration of dignity, self-love and respect among peoples.

Addis Deities
In Addis Ababa. Enjoying a meal, a beer and the sudden presence of melanin Goddesses

Marriage is No Mirage
Reflection on Love, Marriage and raising a family – US suburban style.

For Those of Us with Black Suns.
Written in 2012, when Trayvon Martin was murdered in Florida. Our boys were 10 and 14 years old, and we are always anxious for their safety. It is a constant worry.

Leh Wi Pre
Written in Krio. A prayer and invocation to the Ancestors.

Let Us Pray (Translation)
My Ancestors in heaven, who intercede for us, defend and take care of us

I seek your support, as a child of Pamela and Cyril
Please provide direction, and peace.

Notes

We are descended from the same roots

We share the same heritage through our mothers' umbilical cord
Please heed our cry
You see our struggle
Do not let us fall
We want good health and prosperity forever, to keep the memory of your good deeds alive
I shall always keep my promise to honor our family forever
Thank you for all your blessings.

ENDNOTES

---

[1] **Serra Lyoa.** (Portugese) Original name for Sierra Leone, meaning Lion Mountain

[2] **Kɛkɛ.** Motorized tricycle taxi

[3] **Samba Gɔta.** (Krio) large culverts built to divert water from the hills surrounding Freetown

[4] **Bɔmɛ.** Name/location of Freetown's waste depot

[5] **Tawzin.** (Krio) Thousand

[6] **Rum ɛn Pala.** (Krio) Bedroom and parlor dwelling. Usually with an external shared toilet

[7] **Bata.** (Krio) A plastic jerry Can, usually yellow

[8] **Plasas.** (Krio) Contraction of "Palavar Sauce". A stew made from leaves and palm oil

[9] **Tamatis.** (Krio) Tomato

[10] **Bod Os Dɛm.** (Krio) Wooden (board) houses

[11] **ECOMOG.** Economic Community of West African State Monitoring Group. Soldiers mainly from Nigeria sent on mission to guarantee the peace during the civil war in Sierra Leone

[12] **Poda Poda.** Commercial mini bus

[13] **Kɛkɛ.** Motorized tricycle taxi

[14] **Kɛkɛ.** Motorized tricycle taxi

ENDNOTES

[15] **Poda Poda**. Commercial mini bus

[16] **Kɛkɛ**. Motorized tricycle taxi

[17] **Joblo jabla**. (Krio) Messy. All mixed up

[18] **Sabanɔ**. (Themne) Our Town

[19] **Ɔmɔlankɛ**. (Krio) Cart to carry goods. Pushed manually

[20] **Wetin Du Wi Ba? (Krio)** What's wrong with us?

[21] **bɔt bra, wi nɔr de fil am o.** (Krio) It doesn't bother us at all.

[22] **Kɔlɛ.** (Krio) To be in awe of

[23] **wan place dancing.** (Krio) Staying in place, un-progressive

[24] **dɛn sai wɛ dɛn tai cow, dan de dɔn bɔhku passmak.** (Krio) Refers to a cow pasture. A comfortable place – too many comfortable places

[25] **Leh wi manaj am so.** (Krio) To take things as they are, not to fuss over deficiencies

[26] **all kine bactɔk...ɛn sing dɔn bɔs pan dis.** (Krio) Sarcastic retorts and songs making fun of an issue

[27] **so, so book, wan sabi nɔr de de.** (Krio) Knowledge without experience

[28] **Tumara.** (Krio) Tomorrow

[29] **kolor ɛn im masta.** (Krio) Everyone

[30] **Tem dɔn dɔn pan ple ple.** (Krio) Time to be serious

ENDNOTES

[31] **Bwoi.** (Jamaican Patois) Slang for Boy

[32] **Macru.** (Krio) Yeast infection, with severe itching, usually in children

[33] **Peggy.** (Krio) Sycophant

[34] **34.** Refers to the 34th Regiment Military Hospital in Freetown

[35] **Buga.** A dance denoting power

[36] **Sara.** Sacrifice of an animal in supplication to the Gods

[37] **Alagba Dem.** (Yoruba) Refers to people of influence and wealth

[38] **Oporto.** (Themne, Portugese); Meaning white man or foreigner

[39] **Dunya.** (Themne) Our town

[40] **Look gron good oh.** (Krio) Take heed

[41] **Panbodies.** (Krio) Slum dwelling. Usually made up of Corrugated zinc sheets

[42] **Sobels.** Contraction of Soldier – Rebel

[43] **ECOMOG** – Economic Community of West African State Monitoring Group. Soldiers mainly from Nigeria sent on mission to guarantee peace during the civil war in Sierra Leone

[44] **Lɛ i Pwɛl.** (Krio) Let It Rot

[45] **JCs.** (Krio) Jɛs Cam: Slang for returnees back to Sierra Leone on holiday or short stay

[46] **Sɔriart.** (Krio) Empathetic person

ENDNOTES

[47] **Friends of the Dead.** An informal club of grave diggers and hustlers usually stationed at cemeteries

[48] **Yu Bɔbɔ de.** (Krio) Literally, a greeting of deference and respect to someone older, wealthy or powerful. It is also used in whimsical exaggeration

[49] **Chale.** A term of endearment, usually in greeting. Commonly used in Ghana, West Africa

[50] **We Yon Pɔrsin.** (Krio) A dear friend

[51] **Yu go Soba.** (Krio) You will regret this

[52] **da rop we de bɛn, bɔt nɔ go brok.** (Krio) Refers to a family bonds being accommodating and unbreakable

[53] **ndig-ge ya-ha-lu.** (Mende) Greet all those in the other realm

[54] **Bwel Soup.** (Krio) A spicy hot broth with fish, pork and beef

[55] **Plasas.** (Krio) Contraction of "Palavar Sauce". A stew made from leaves and palm oil

[56] **Kortoh.** (Krio) Islamic teacher. But Fula traders were commonly referred to as such

www.ingramcontent.com/pod-product-compliance
Ingram Content Group UK Ltd.
Pitfield, Milton Keynes, MK11 3LW, UK
UKHW020244240426
12048UKWH00026B/1593